THE AWAKENING OF FAITH

THE AWAKENING OF FAITH IN THE MAHAYANA DOCTRINE-THE NEW BUDDHISM

BY THE
PATRIARCH ASHVAGOSHA

Who died about A.D. 100

Translated into Chinese by Paramartha (Chen Ti)
Who lived in the Liang dynasty A.D. (502-555)

Translated into English in 1894 By
REV. TIMOTHY RICHARD, LITT. D.
Assisted by Mr. Yang Wen Hwui

GYAN

Published by

Gyan Publishing House
5, Ansari Road
Daryaganj, New Delhi-110002
Phone: 011-47034999, 9811692060
E-mail: books@gyanbooks.com

Distribution Network
gyanbooks.com
India, USA, Canada, UK, Australia, France

ISBN : 978-81-212-2380-5 (PB)
First Published, 1907

2nd Impression 2021

Printed at: Gyan Press, Delhi.

The
Awakening of Faith
Author: Patriarch Ashvagosha

THE AWAKENING OF FAITH

IN THE

MAHAYANA DOCTRINE—THE NEW BUDDHISM

BY THE

PATRIARCH ASHVAGOSHA

Who died about A. D. 100

Translated into Chinese by Paramartha (Chen Ti 眞諦)
Who lived in the Liang dynasty A. D. (502-555)

Translated into English in 1894 by
Rev. TIMOTHY RICHARD, LITT.D.
Assisted by Mr. Yang Wên Hwui

SHANGHAI
CHRISTIAN LITERATURE SOCIETY,

1907

ASHVAGOSHA—THE NEIGHING HORSE.

CONTENTS

PAGES

Translator's Introduction - - - - - - - v

Translator's Synopsis - - - - - - - - - XVII

The Opening Hymn - - - - - - - - - - XXVI

CHAPTER.—I

Reasons for writing the Book - - - - - - 1

CHAPTER.—II

The Fundamental Doctrine of the New Buddhism—the Mahayana Faith - - - - 3

CHAPTER.—III

Exposition of the Faith - - - - - - - 4

CHAPTER.—IV

The Practice of the Faith - - - - - - - 35

CHAPTER.—V

The Advantages of the Faith - - - - - - 44

TRANSLATOR'S INTRODUCTION

1. One of the great Books of the World.

大乘起信論

This is the title of one of the most important books in the world. A Japanese scholar has translated it *The Awakening of Faith*. It might also be rendered *The Mahayana Faith* or *The Faith of the New Buddhism*. Its importance is apparent when we consider the fact that of the 26,000 Buddhist monks and nuns in Japan no less than 17,000 of them belong to the Pure Land School and the True School, which regard this book as their fountain and origin.

Its importance is still more apparent when we consider that its doctrines are the fundamental ones of the Mahayana Faith, which is by far the chief school of Buddhism, not only in Japan, but also in China, where are the great majority of the Buddhists of the world. If we estimate the value of books by the number of adherents to their doctrines, then, after the Bible, the Koran, the Confucian Classics, and the Vedas, this volume, about the size of the Gospel of Mark, ranks next, or fifth, among the sacred books of the world.

The great value of the book is also apparent when we remember that the Eastern world had been driven to general despair by the atheistic doctrines of primitive Buddhism, called the Hinayana School, and that it was by the doctrines of this book, which gave rise to the Mahayana School of New Buddhism, that a gospel of great hope was preached to the greater part of the Eastern Asiatic continent. Its new doctrines were that of the One Soul immanent for good in all the universe, that of a Divine Helper of men, of individual immortality and growth in the likeness of God, of the importance of faith in God to produce good works and that of the willingness of the best spirits to make sacrifices to save others—the very subjects which in these modern days still occupy the attention of the most thoughtful men of the world.

The book is Brahministic and Buddhistic, Indian and Western in some aspects of philosophic thought. It is profoundly philosophic, reminding one strongly of Hegel, Berkeley and G. Gore in the earlier part, and is as hard to understand as Bishop Butler's famous Analogy; yet very practical in the latter part, therefore it has great importance arising from its high and extensive range of view.

If it be, as it is more and more believed that the Mahayana Faith is not Buddhism, properly so-called, but an Asiatic form of the same Gospel of our Lord and Saviour Jesus Christ, in Buddhistic nomenclature, differing from the old Buddhism just as the new Testament differs from the old, then it commands a world-wide interest, for in it we find an adaptation of Christianity to ancient thought in Asia, and the deepest bond of union between the different races of the East and the West, *viz.*, the bond of a common religion. Both Christianity and the New Buddhism hold to the transcendent and the immanent forms of God; but the East emphasises more of the immanent form while the West emphasises more of the transcendent. The almost universal reception of the doctrines contained in this book by both the East and the West constitutes to my mind its highest claim to our attention; for thereby we are brought face to face with a solution of the stupendous practical problem of uniting all races in one bond of religious charity!

II. The Evolution and Devolution of Buddhism.

The evolution of Buddhism is seen in the new Buddhism superseding the old, and the devolution in the attempt by later writers to combine the primitive with the advanced, an absurd anachronism and impossibility.

This will be apparent from the study of the different schools of Buddhism.

The most common division of Buddhism is that into the smaller (*Hinayana*), or Primitive Buddhism, and the greater (*Mahayana*) or Advanced Buddhism.

During Gautama Buddha's life there were no books of his teaching written, but according to a Japanese book on Buddhism called *Pa-chung-kang-yao*, 八宗綱要 published in A. D. 1319, tradition says that during the first 400 years after Gautama Buddha's death (B. C. 543) the *Hinayana* school flourished greatly while the *Mahayana* was not known. But 500 years after Buddha's death, Maming (Ashvagosha) wrote the book on *The Mahayana Faith*. The *Mahayana* school then began to flourish everywhere, while the *Hinayana* went under a cloud. This makes, the rise of the *Mahayana* school contemporaneous with the rise of Christianity.

Besides this broad division into the *Hinayana* and the *Mahayana* schools, there are other divisions of Buddhism which are interesting to know, as they indicate the development and growth of religious ideas in the Buddhist religion, just as in the Christian and in every other religion, and also their decay when Buddhist learning was neglected. For example, in China the Tientai school of Buddhism, with its headquarters in the mountains of Chêkiang province, divides Buddhism into four schools, *viz*:—

1.—The *Tsang Chiao* 藏教, Primitive Buddhism (*i.e.* the *Hinayana*).

2.—*Tung Chiao* 通教, Buddhism in a transition state.

3.—*Pieh Chiao* 別教, New Buddhism (*i.e.* the *Mahayana*).

4.—*Yuan Chiao* 圓教, the complete religion of all the schools.

The Hsien Shou 賢首, School of Buddhism—founded by followers of Fa Tsang, called also Hsien Shou, the third Patriarch after Wên Shu Pusa, the great Buddhist saint of Wutai, north of the province of Shansi, who died A.D. 627 and is specially worshipped by the Mongols—divides Buddhism into five schools, *viz*:—

1.—The *Siao Chiao* 小教, or Primitive Buddhism (the *Hinayana*).

2—*Shih Chiao* 始教, or the Beginning of True Religion (transition state).

3.—The *Chung Chiao* 終教, or the Final Development of the True Religion (the *Mahayana*).

4.—The *Tun Chiao* 頓教, or the School of Meditation, founded by the last Buddhist patriarch Ta Mo, not mentioned separately in the Tientai classification. Ta Mo, A. D. 529.

5.—The *Yuan Chiao* 圓教, or the Complete Religion of all the schools.

Generally speaking the classifications of both agree. But the Tientai school, south of the province of Chekiang, regard the *Lien-hua-king* 蓮華經 or the *Lotus Classic* as their chief scripture, while the Hsien Shou school on the north regards the *Hua-yen-king* 華嚴經 as their chief scripture. But both these chief scriptures are said to have their origin in the *Chi-hsin-lun* 起信論, the book which we now translate under the name of the *New Buddhist Faith*, called in Sanskrit the *Mahayana sraddhotpada sastra*. These classifications are rather ancient. There is a great dearth of books on the subject of modern schools of Buddhism showing the decline of Buddhism in China during the last two dynasties, but there are writers now at work to give the later history of Buddhism in China and to bring it down to date.

In Japan while Buddhism is divided into the two great schools—the *True School*, by which one seeks salvation by reliance on self, and the *Pure Land School*, by which one seeks salvation by the help of God—all Buddhists are now sub-divided into twelve sects. An outline of each of these was given by one of the leading men in each school, and Bunyiu Nanjio, M.A. (Oxon), the ablest Sanskrit scholar in Japan, translated them into English and published them in 1886 under the name of *A Short History of the Twelve Japanese Buddhist Sects*.

Most of these sects, like the Romanists, forbid their priests to marry; but others, like the Protestants, give their priests perfect liberty to marry or not as they please. Some sects expect to work out their own salvation with fear and trembling, saying that whatsoever a man sows that shall he also reap—the Karma of the old Buddhism—while other sects say that repentance and faith in God can far outstrip all independent efforts at salvation. Some of the sects insist on incessant study and like the Positivists expect their followers to be encyclopædias of all knowledge, while others again are only expected to repeat O-mi-to-Fo, like ourselves in our Western religions, who think the "Hail Mary" or "Only Believe" sufficient doctrines equally absurd or profound according to our standpoint of observing them or of using them. Thus we see a striking parallelism in the development of religion in the West and in the East—signs of life as well as of decay.

III.—How I came to translate this book.

The story is of no small interest. In 1884 I visited Nanking in company with my revered friend, David Hill, to see the Viceroy, and tried to persuade him to interest himself in securing religious freedom for Christians and immunity from persecution. Whilst there, I sought for some Buddhist books which I could not procure in the North of China. I learnt that a Buddhist Book Society had been started in Nanking, Soochow, and Hangchow, three of the leading cities in Central China, in order to replace those destroyed during the Tai Ping Rebellion. Of the three societies, the most important was that at Nanking, and the prime mover of the whole three societies lived there. His name was Yang Wên Hui. I called on him and found him the most intelligent Buddhist I had ever met. He had been several years in Europe as treasurer to the Chinese Embassy when Marquis Tseng represented China in England and France. Mr. Yang had had interviews with Max Müller and Julien and Bunyiu Nanjio of Tokio, who had studied under Max Müller. Thus, besides being well acquainted with the Buddhist authorities in China, he was personally acquainted with the best authorities in Europe and Japan. Mr. Yang was not a Buddhist priest, but a Confucianist with the B. A. (siutsai) degree and was only a lay Buddhist.

I said to him, "How is it that you, with a Confucian degree, should have ever become a Buddhist?" His answer was striking: "I am surprised that you, a missionary, should ask me that question, for you must know that Confucianism shirks some of the most important questions. It only deals with human affairs now, not with the superhuman." "But do you mean to say that Buddhism answers those questions?" He said, "Yes." "Where?" I asked again. He answered, "In a book called the Awakening of Faith. That book converted me from Confucianism to Buddhism." "Have you that book for sale here?" I asked. "Yes," he replied, and brought the book and laid it in my hands. Finding him to be most thoroughly conversant with the relative value of the various Buddhist books, I asked him to select for me some dozen works which he considered most important. Having paid for them, I returned to my inn. Shortly after, the box containing all my purchases arrived. I looked for the book on the *Awakening of Faith* and began reading it and sat up reading it till the small hours of the morning. I cried to my friend Hill, who was also sitting up late at work, "This is a Christian book and most interesting." "Christian?" my friend cried with great doubt.

"You are reading your own thoughts into the book!" "Well then," I said, "how do you explain these passages?" pointing to some to which there was no ready explanation.

Three months later I was in a bookseller's shop in Edinburgh, and looking through his new books I came across Beal's little book on Buddhism lately published. Turning up a certain chapter in it, I found that he referred to the Awakening of Faith as a Pseudo-Christian book which it was desirable to have translated.

Years passed by. In 1891 I was transferred to Shanghai. Shortly after, I met my friend Mr. Yang again, and I told him that I had read the Awakening of Faith with great interest, but that frequently I came across philosophical terms which no existing dictionary explained and which even excellent Chinese scholars could not explain. If he could spare some of his time to come to Shanghai, I would spare some of my time to translate it with his help. He readily agreed and was delighted to have the book made known to those interested in Buddhism in the West. Thus the book was translated into English in 1894. But it was not published then, as I wished to have leisure time to revise it before publication. That time of leisure has never come. Six years later (1900) Suzuki's translation into English was published by the Open Court, Chicago. His translation bears the mark of one who has spent much study on the subject. In his introduction, he quotes a large number of different authorities about Ashvagosha. But as he approaches the subject from the non-Christian point of view, the light which comes from a comparison between it and Christianity is denied him. He dwells more on his philosophical "suchness" or on his psychological theory of "triple personality" and only on one religious characteristic "faith," apparently unconscious of its incalculable importance as a religions eirenicon between the East and the West. Though I have had no time to revise this translation of mine, I publish it because I believe it is capable of producing brotherhood amongst men, and mutual respect among religious teachers, when it is properly interpreted in the light of Christianity.

IV.—Unity in Diversity.

In the Diamond Sutra, which is one of the most popular of all the Buddhist Sutras and most widely used throughout China, there is a very remarkable passage attributed to Gautama Buddha in the Sixth chapter. It is to this effect: "Five hundred years after my death there will arise a religious prophet who will lay the foundation of his teaching, not on one, two, three, four, or five Buddhas, nor even on ten thousand Buddhas, but on the Fountain of all the Buddhas; when that one comes, have faith in Him, and you will receive incalculable blessings." Now since it is well known that Jesus Christ and Ashvagosha did appear some 500 years after Buddha, this is one of the most remarkable prophecies in the whole range of Sacred Literature. But to return to the *Awakening of Faith*. It is of immense interest and importance to find in this book alone the following striking contrasts between the old Buddhism and the new Buddhism.

1.—The Old Buddhism was atheistic; the New is theistic.

2.—The Old Buddhism trusted in salvation by one's own efforts (Karma); the New trusted in the help of God as well.

3.—The Old Buddhism believed in retirement from the evil world; the New believed in living in the world and in saving others as the highest virtue.

4.—The Old Buddhism believed in countless transmigrations before the many could be delivered; the

New believed in passing into Paradise at once without any rounds of transmigration.

No one who is acquainted with the characteristics of Christianity can read these things without being struck with the remarkable similarity of these five points of the new Buddhism with it ; nay, they are exactly the same so far as they go. Buddhism and Christianity at first contact in modern days were mutually hostile to one another. But when the earnest students of both religions penetrated through the different forms and nomenclature into the deep internal meaning of all, they found not only that they aimed at the same thing, the salvation of the world, but that many of their chief teachings were common to both. They no longer feared each other as foes, but helped each other as friends.

V.—Common origin in Babylon

It is getting clearer each year now, that these common doctrines of New Buddhism and Christianity were not borrowed from one another, but that both came from a common source, Babylonia, where some of the Jewish prophets wrote their glorious visions of the kingdom of God that was to come. Babylon then had much intercourse with Western India and Persia, as well as with Judæa, Egypt and Greece. From this centre these great life-giving inspiring truths were carried like seeds into both the East and West where they were somewhat modified under different conditions.

It is also getting clearer each year that different truths, wherever found, cannot be antagonistic. They do not neutralise, but complement each other ; they do not destroy, but fulfil one another.

VI.—Ashvagosha

The various accounts of the life of Ashvagosha are so contradictory and many, so full of impossible legends, that it is difficult to know how to separate the false from the true. But all are agreed :—

that he was a Brahman who was converted to Buddhism ;

that he travelled extensively in Central India and later in Northern India and that he largely describes things of Western India in his Book of Great Glory ;

that he was contemporary with, if not adviser of King Kanishka of North-Western India, who lived in the first century of the Christian era, and probably attended the third great council of Buddhism held in Kashmir ;

that he was the founder of the New Buddhism, often called the Mahayana School, or the Northern Buddhism ;

that seven other works of his have been translated into Chinese, one of which is a celebrated life of Buddha translated by Beal.

His conversion as given by Suzuki is almost as striking as that which Yang related to me about his own conversion. The day had come for a public discussion of religion, as was common in India at that time, and Ashvagosha and Pareva were to be the debaters. Ashvagosha said, "The one unable to answer shall have his tongue cut out." The other replied, "No, he shall become a disciple of the winner." Then he asked Ashvagosha, "What shall we have to do in order to keep the kingdom in perfect peace, to have the king live long, to let the people enjoy abundance and prosperity, all free from evils and catastrophies?" Not being able to answer this, Ashvagosha became the other's disciple.

How to bring down high dogma to practical life for the permanent good of all classes remains still the great problem of life, philosophy, and religion.

VII.—The Text

This book on the Awakening of Faith is mentioned in an old catalogue of Buddhist Scriptures in the T'ang dynasty. I asked a friend in India to try and procure me the copy of the original in Sanskrit, but he has not succeeded. This Chinese version of it was made by the Buddhist missionary, Paramartha (Chen-ti 眞諦) who lived in China in the Liang dynasty, A.D. 502-555.

VIII.—Translation

It is a common error of translators to translate the same word always by the same word. As the same word in different connections often has different meanings and the translated word, however literal, does not always cover exactly the same amount of meaning as the original, I have endeavoured to give the true meaning of the original, although the English rendering may be by different words in different places. That is why I have rendered the term 眞如 by True Form, True Likeness, True Reality, Archetype, and other terms, rather than by any unfamiliar term, as likely to give a more correct idea of the original to the beginner in the study of Buddhism.

IX.—Conclusion

The reader who is acquainted with the low state of Buddhism in China to-day may naturally ask, since the New Buddhism was so full of such high teaching on some of the greatest problems of life and since it was so flourishing for many centuries, why is its glory departed? The answer is, besides what is given in Section II, that it is largely for want of proper education in its religion. The same is true of Taoism. It is only the Confucianists who have a grand system of education, and with that all power and influence is theirs, while the other religions have only reaped weakness and shame in consequence of their ignorance. The term Julai, instead of being rendered by Tathagata, another foreign term, is best rendered by Messiah in English, as it means the True Form become incarnate.

TRANSLATOR'S SYNOPSIS

CHAPTER.—I

Reasons for writing this book— 1

QUESTION 1.—Why write the book?

ANSWER:

A.—Not to get fame, but to give happiness to a world of sorrow.

B.—To lead men to the right through Ju Lai the Incarnate Transcendent One.

C.—To lead the best men to the Mahayana Faith or the New Buddhism.

D.—To lead less noble men to have some faith.

E.—To show how to get rid of all error.

F.—To rid worldly men and those of the two lower schools (the Hinayana and middle schools) of error.

G.—To show men how to see God (Buddha).

H.—To show the benefits of this Faith.

QUESTION 2.—As the Sutras explain all this, why write a new book?

ANSWER 2.—To give a comprehensive view of the whole to intelligent men. 2

CHAPTER.—II

The fundamental doctrine of the Mahayana Faith: 3

A.—Its nature—the Soul of all.

B.—Its attributes—all pervading.

Chapter.—III

Exposition of the Faith— 4

A.—By Definitions.

B.—By correcting heresies.

C.—By showing the steps of progress.

D.—By Definitions. The One Soul has two aspects.

1. —The Eternal transcendent one—beyond all language.

Question 3.—How then can any follow it? 5

Answer. Though beyond language yet conceivable.

A.—It is not like ordinary realities.

B.—It is nevertheless the most real of all.

2. —As the temporary immanent one—in all living beings. 6

A.—The Mahayana Faith has some infinite or divine knowledge

In the original state,

In the various states of acquired knowledge,

Behind thought and intermixed with the experience.

(1.) In this Original or Divine light there is 8

(*a.*) Pure Wisdom,

(*b.*) Wonderful goodness.

(2.) The attributes of this Original or Divine light are 9

(*a.*) Infinite recreation of the Eternal Unity as extensive as space and like a bright reflecting mirror.

(*b.*) Infinite revelation of the Eternal energy—a reflector of the real influences.

(c.) Infinite revelation of righteous law—a reflector of that which is without sorrow or hindrance.

(d.) Infinite revelation of love — reflector which shines on all living beings.

b. The Mahayana Faith has acquired knowledge.

(1.) Producing three states of acquired knowledge 10

(a.) Sensation,

(b.) Consciousness,

(c.) Perception.

Corresponding to a classification into six stages of

(a.) Consciousness,

(b.) Sensation,

(c.) Perception,

(d.) Differentiation,

(e.) Will,

(f.) Reflection.

(2.) Showing two different conditions— 11

The Eternal and Acquired.

(a.) The same nature just as a fragment of pottery and all the pottery are of clay.

(b.) But different forms just as the clay is made into different vessels.

(3.) Producing the five kinds of thoughts—

(a.) Faculty of sensation, 10

(b.) ,, ,, consciousness,

(c.) ,, perception,

(d.) ,, conception,

(e.) ,, will.

(4.) Producing the opinions of imperfect knowledge.

Those ways which lead the soul astray are six, viz :—

(*a.*) Through false perception,
(*b.*) Through false affections,
(*c.*) Through analogy of various knowledge,
(*d.*) Through analogy of objective forms,
(*e.*) Through innacurate perception,
(.) Through innacurate sensation.

(5.) Having two states, the rough and the fine. 15

QUESTION 4.—If the soul ends, how does it continue? If it continues, how does it end?

ANSWER. What ends is only the state of the soul, not the soul itself.

(6.) Having four influences incessantly at work—the true, the untrue, the confused, the false objective.

(*a.*) The misleading influence- 16
a.a. of the false world,
b.b. of false opinions,
c.c. of ignorance. 17

(*b.*) The constant purfying influences
a.a. of the imperfect good opinions,
b.b. of the transcendent. 18

(I) Directly by its own nature.

QUESTION 5.—As all have the transcendent what need of faith and practice?

ANSWER. It is because imperfect knowledge differs

(II) Indirectly by the powers of other beings 19
(*a.a.a.*) Through different motives,
(*b.b.b.*) Through the same transcendent motives. 20

(III) By contrast and by example.
(*c.*) One ends, the other never ends. 21

(7.) Having the Transcendent's own nature and state.

QUESTION 6.—As the transcendent is independent of all states, how do you speak of all kinds of blessings and possibilities?

ANSWER. Although it has these blessings, it is independent of any state.

(8.) Having the transcendent in action—Buddha's vows begin here. 22

(*a.*) Has the faculty of distinguishing between good and evil—the Regenerated Spirit (Ying Shen). 23

(*b.*) Has the faculty of conscious indwelling—the Inspired Spirit (Pao Shen).

(*c.*) Has the faculty of knowing suffering. 24

(*d.*) Has the faculty of perceiving the Divine Spirit (Fa Shên).

(*e.*) Has finally the faculty beyond human experience—the Buddha experience.

QUESTION 7.—If the Buddhas are independent of all visible states, how can they manifest themselves?

ANSWER. The spiritual state is the Soul of all the visible, therefore can manifest itself in the invisible.

(9.) Being shown in leaving the immanent for the transcendent. 25

B.—By correcting heresies

1. About terms such as

a. That Julai is space,

b. That nirvana and the transcendent are intangible, 26

c. That Julai embraces matter and spirit, therefore these cannot be cured, *d.* That as Julai embraces everything, therefore it embraces life and death,

e. That the joys of nirvana come to an end when Julai comes from heaven to save men. 27

2. About the relation of the transcendent to the immanent being inimical,

3. About purity and defilement being absolute, not relative.

C.—By showing the different steps of progress— 28

1. Growth of faith depends on men and character.

a. Faith is not mere goodness which may fail.

b. Faith is threefold—is based on the transcendent rejoices in all good, and helps to save. 29

QUESTION 8.—As men and the transcendent are the same, what need is there for practice?

ANSWER. Like a precious stone from a quarry, it must be polished.

c. Faith employs four means of progress. 30

(1.) Cultivates the study of the root of all things,

(2.) Prevents evil,

(3.) Grows in goodness,

(4.) Grows in the desire of the salvation of all beings.

d. Faith-fruits manifested in self-sacrifices—the Regenerated Spirit (Ying-Shen). 31

e. Faith descends to save others.

. Faith never fails because of difficulties.

2. Growth in intelligent practice of the five Paramitas (Great Virtues)— 32

a. Paramita of Charity,

b. Paramita of Discipline (Holy Life),

c. Paramita of Endurance,

d. Paramita of Perseverance,

e. Paramita of Unchangeableness,

f. Paramita of Wisdom in discerning what is good and evil.

3. Growth in attainments—

a. The Pusa disciple (Saint) becomes able to reach all places to support the enlightened.

b. This Growth of the Pusa is threefold—the transcendent ideal, the means used and the perfection attained. 33

c. This perfection is Buddhahood (Divinity).

QUESTION 9.—To comprehend all beings in all the worlds, how can any get this seed of wisdom?

ANSWER. By obtaining the omniscience that is independent of the senses and is in all minds. 34

QUESTION 10.—If the Buddhas (Divine Emanations) are incarnate everywhere to save mankind, why do you say that most people cannot see them?

ANSWER. Only those pure like a bright mirror are able to reflect and see such.

CHAPTER.—IV

The practice of the Faith— 35

A. How to practise Charity,

B. How to practise complete Ethics, 36

C. How to practise enduring wrong,

D. How to practise perseverance,

E. How to practise checking vain thought and getting sound reflection. 37

1. Preventing vain thought—sitting in quietness and then

a. Think of the means of checking vain thoughts till you get transcendent peace, 38

b. Learn that the peace of all in heaven and earth is the same,

c. Think when tempted of the One Eternal Soul, 39

d. Find out the ten advantages of peace in this life. 40

2. Reflect

a. That nothing created lasts long, 41

b. That life is full of sorrow,

c. That the present self is not the real self, the past is a dream, the present a lightning flash, the future smoke,

d. That all living beings are stained,

e. That existence down all ages is marred by sorrow and therefore to be pitied, 42

f. That a great vow should be made to save others,

g. That the vow should be carried out in practice.

3. Check vain thoughts and reflect at the same time and at all times.

4. Reflect on Amitabha (God) so as not to lose faith. 43

CHAPTER.—V

Advantages of the Faith— 44

A. Generally it will obtain the very highest doctrine.

B. Will attain to Buddhahood (the Divine state).

C. An hour of faith surpasses a universe of good works.

D. The advantages are incalculable, for eternity is not long enough to calculate them.

E. Unbelievers and revilers have no hope of salvation.

F. It is by means of this Faith that the Buddhas and the Pusas of the past and present have attained and are attaining their pure faith, therefore follow it! 45

The closing hymn.

Opening Hymn

I yield my life to the All,
To the ALL SOUL, full of good,
In wisdom all complete,
In power all divine,
In pity–would save all.

To LAW which does embody
The Archetype of all.

To CHURCH which does contain
The Archetype in Seed,

That men may be delivered
From doubt and evil ways;
Get Faith in the great School
Perpetuating God!

CHAPTER.—I

Reasons for Writing the book.

QUESTION 1.—What are the reasons for writing this book?

ANSWER 1.—The reasons for it are eight.

A.—Generally speaking, it is to induce all living beings to depart from the way of all sorrow and to obtain the highest happiness, instead of seeking the glitter of fame and wealth of this world.

B.—It is to make clear the fundamental idea of the incarnate god (Ju Lai) in man, and to lead all beings in the right way avoiding error.

C.—It is to lead those ripe in goodness to continue in the Mahayana Faith without failing.

D.—It is to enable those in whom the root of goodness is very small to cultivate faith more and more.

E.—It is to show how to remove evil hindrances and to strengthen well the mind, to keep far from mad pride and to see through the deceits of vice.

F.—It is to show how to study and correct the errors of ordinary men and the errors of the two inferior schools (the Hinayana or elementary school and the Madhyi-mayna or middle School of Buddhism).

G.—It is to show the means by which one may ascend to the abode of God (Buddha) and never lose faith.

H.—It is to show the benefits of this Faith and to exhort men to practise it.

These are the main reasons for writing this book.

QUESTION 2—As the Sutras, or classic Buddhist Scriptures, explain these things fully, what need is there of repeating them?

ANSWER 2.—Although the Sutras have discussed these things, yet as men's abilities and attainments are different, the reception of instruction is necessarily different. When the Incarnate god (Ju Lai) was on earth, all men were able to understand Him. His body and mind far excelled those of all other men. When he delivered his perfect words all living beings, though different in kind, understood him alike, and therefore there was no need of explanation.

But after Ju Lai's death we find that some men, after widely reading the Sacred Scriptures, have the power unaided to understand them ; we find that others after only hearing a little of the Sacred Scriptures have the power unaided to understand much ; we also find that some have not sufficient intelligence to understand the Scriptures unassisted by extensive explanations, whilst we find that others dislike voluminous writings and prefer a terse style which embraces many principles and which they are able to understand.

Thus this book is written for the last class of men which desire to know the general principles of the great and profound Law of Ju Lai with its infinite applications.

CHAPTER.—II

The Fundamental Doctrine of the Mahayana Faith.

Having explained the object of writing this book we now proceed to consider the fundamental doctrine of the Mahayana Faith. The great school (Mahayana) speaks of the Eternal Soul of the universe, His nature and His attributes.

A.—By His nature is meant the Soul of all living beings. The soul embraces that of saved and of unsaved beings and it is this universal Soul that characterises the great school. For it is the Archetype's True Eternal Form which is the nature of the Mahayana Faith; and the Archytype's temporary form in life which is able to make manifest the nature, form and use of the Mahayana Faith.

B.—As to the attributes of this Soul they are three. The first is the vastness of its nature. All things are originally one and the same and an eternally fixed quantity in the True Form. The second covers its vast manifestations. In the person of Ju Lai, the True Form, there are infinite possibilities stored up as in a womb. The third is its vast power. It is able to produce all good among all classes of living beings saved and unsaved.

All the enlightened Buddhas follow this Mahayana Faith and all the Chief Apostles (Pusas) attain to the perfection of Ju Lai by the methods of this Faith of the New Buddhism.

CHAPTER.—III

Expositions of the Mahayana Faith.

These expositions are of three kinds.

A.—Those about the meaning.

B.—Those about the correction of erroneous conceptions.

C.—Those about the different steps of progress.

As to the meaning of the One Soul there are two aspects.

1.—One is the eternal transcendent Soul.

2.—The other is the temporary immanent Soul.

These two aspects embrace everything for they are really one.

1.—The eternal state of the Soul.

The Soul or mind of the True Form is the great essence of the invisible and the visible worlds. As to the nature of this One soul it is the same in all forms. To think it is different in different forms is only a false notion of the world. Once we penetrate beyond forms it is discovered that all the different forms of the universe are not real differences of soul at all, but different manifestations of one real power, hence it has always been impossible to speak adequately, to name correctly or to think correctly of this One Soul, the real essence of things, which is unchangeable and indestructible. We therefore name it the TRUE ESSENCE OR THE LIKENESS OR THE TRUE FORM. But all nomenclature of these matters is imperfect and if one follows superficial thought, the true meaning cannot be found out. Even though we call it the True Likeness, it has no form. It is because language in its extremity fails us that we coin a new term to avoid ordinary ideas. But the nature of the Archetype is a reality that cannot be destroyed, for all things are true though they cannot be truly pointed out to the senses, and all forms are really only different manifestations of the one True Form. It should be remembered that this is beyond ordinary language and beyond ordinary thought, therefore we name it the True Form.

QUESTION 3.—How then are men to follow and obey and find the way to this True Form of things?

ANSWER 3.—One must know that although one cannot speak of this adequately, as it is beyond all expression, and although one cannot think of this adequately, as it is beyond all thought, yet we call this state the seeking after; and that when we leave ordinary thought of these things we are entering into the gate of knowledge. Next when using words to discuss the True Form it may be spoken of in two ways, viz., first as the unreal as compared with ordinary realities, in order eventually to show its reality; secondly as the only real as compared with ordinary realities, because it has a nature of its own full of infinite possibilities.

A.—First then the Unreal.

When we speak of the unreal we mean that which has never been defiled, which is separate from all existing forms and which common men cannot understand.

We should know the nature of this True Form. It has no form, yet it is not formless. This is not saying that it is without any form, but that it is not the ordinary form. It is composed of neither ordinary, existing nor non-existing forms. It is neither one definite form nor is it the many different forms. This is not saying that it has no definite form and that it is not in the many different forms. It is neither one nor many different forms. Generally speaking, as the world has many different notions, all false, we call this the Unreal Empty Form. But if false notions are given up, this is then the most Real.

B.—Secondly the Real.

When we speak of the Real we have already explained that the True Form is apparently Unreal but true; in other words that it is the true mind, eternal, and unchanged, full of purity, therefore we call it the Real

One. But it has no form. When the imperfect notions of things are given up, then alone can we verify this truth.

2.—The Eternal Soul immanent in the temporary.

The temporary arises from the forces of the Eternal Ju Lai, the uniting of the eternal with the temporary. It is neither the same nor different, but we call it the Natural state of man. This natural state has two meanings, viz., that which embraces all things and that which produces all things : the first is called the Infinite enlightenment, the second the Finite enlightenment.

A.—Infinite Enlightenment.

By infinite enlightenment is meant that which has no false notions and is infinite like space, one with the True Form as in instinct and intuition. This is the natural state of the Incarnate True Form (Ju Lai) and is called the original state of enlightenment. This is to distinguish it from acquired enlightenment which cultivates that infinite enlightenment, for the two have the same thing in common though it is only in part. Where there is the original infinite enlightenment there exists finite enlightenment in those who seek after it. Where there exists finite enlightenment, there is more enlightenment to be acquired.

Again, when one attains to the original enlightenment it is called the perfect enlightenment. When one has not attained to the original enlightenment it is not perfect enlightenment.

For example, when an ordinary man discovers that his former ideas were wrong and is able to prevent such ideas arising any more, such knowledge on his part, though it might be called a kind of enlightenment is only finite.

Or when those learned in the wisdom of the two lower Schools (the Primary and Secondary, or smaller and middle) or such Pusa Apostles as are beginners in the Mahayana school are enlightened so as to know that there is in one sense a difference and in another no difference between these two classes of ideas, we call their knowledge partial enlightenment.

Or when those, such as the Pusas who have arrived at different stages of attainment, are enlightened to know that there is in one sense a resting place and in another sense no rest, in order to distinguish things more clearly their knowledge is called partial enlightenment.

Or when the Pusas have arrived at the highest attainment with all the means of deliverance completed and their thoughts exactly in accordance with the Original Enlightenment, and are enlightened to know that when the false notions began, these had no real beginning, yet in order to escape far from microscopic anxious thought of things, they are able to see the true nature of the One Mind. This state is the eternal one which we call the perfect enlightenment. Therefore the Sutra says that when one can apprehend that which is behind thought, one is on the way to Buddhist wisdom!

Again, as to the beginning of imperfect notions in the mind of men, these have no beginning. But when we speak of their beginning, we mean that they arise without thought, therefore are not called enlightened, as they have not exercised thought. As each thought has been transmitted without interruption from the beginning and men's minds have not been able to free themselves from this, the imperfect notions have been said to be without beginning and to be finite enlightenment. If we meet a man without these thoughts, we shall then know the different stages in the development of the mind, such as beginning, resting satisfied, considering ending because without thought he knows that there is really no difference in kind between the enlightened neophyte's enlightenment and the original enlightenment. For the four states are co-existent and not independent, but are originally all alike—different stages of one and the same enlightenment.

(1.) Next, original enlightenment in men appears according to the different degrees of confusion in two different states, but not separate from the original enlightenment. These different states are the state of pure wisdom and the state of unspeakable blessing where things are incomprehensible.

(*a.*) The state of pure wisdom is that which exists when under the transforming influence of the True Form one cultivates one's nature according to the True Form till all departments of deliverance are completed, when one reaches the state where the temporary gives way to the eternal and is grafted on to the eternal Mind, manifesting itself in the three spiritual institutions—of Buddha (Godhead), of Law, and of Priesthood, hence called the perfect and pure wisdom, because all who are dependent on the senses alone are unenlightened. Those in the? unenlightened state do not depart from the nature of enlightenment; they are neither destructible so long as they depend on the Original Enlightenment nor indestructible when independent of that. Just as the Water in the Ocean, on account of wind, forms itself into waves, wind and waves being inseparable, and yet motion is not an attribute of water, (for if the wind ceases the waves also cease) but the fluid nature of water remains indestructible; so the true nature of man is a clear pure mind. Though on account of the rise of the wind of finite enlightenment the pure mind is moved, the pure mind and the finite knowledge in man's heart are unseen and inseparable but this mind's nature is not finite enlightenment. If the finite enlightenment ceases then the imperfect notions will cease, and the wise nature remains indestructible.

(*b.*) The state of unspeakable blessing is the practical, when it follows pure wisdom and is able to do all sorts of wonderful things, being called the state of infinite blessings, unceasing and natural. In proportion to the natural goodness it abounds in all kinds of blessings according to the need of all.

(2.) Next consider the attributes of this Enlightenment. They are four great ones, infinite as space and clear as a mirror.

(*a*.) Infinite light of the Eternal (Real Emptiness). It is very different from all thought and form. It cannot be made apparent and enlightenment cannot reveal it to the unenlightened.

(*b*.) Infinite light of energy which influences things and which is called the unseen forces (not Real Emptiness). All appearances in the world are brought about by this. They are without appearing and disappearing, without loss or destruction, eternal in the One Mind. All existence is but the true nature of this Mind. Moreover all kinds of defilement cannot defile this. Its nature of wisdom is unchanged, full of perfect energy, influencing all men.

(*c*.) Infinite light of the law of deliverance called the invariable law of Salvation (not unreal Law), which sets aside the hindrances of pessimism and the hindrances to ordinary wisdom and leads one out of the state where the mortal and the immortal are combined so as to get into the perfect free light of life.

(*d*.) The infinite light of practice, called deliverance according to the law, shining on the minds of all living beings, leading them to practise goodness by methods suitable to their needs.

B.—Finite Enlightenment or acquired knowledge.

This is not like the knowledge of the Eternal that there is only one way: hence finite enlightenment shows itself in many forms of existence. These forms have no independent existence separated from the original enlightenment. Just as with a man who has lost his way, his losing of the way depends on his original knowledge of his course (for if he had no idea of the way at first, he could not be said to have lost it) so with men, it is because they have the idea of enlightenment that they know they are unenlightened. If they had no idea of enlightenment in the abstract they could not be said to be altogether unenlightened. From imperfect ideas of unenlightenment men are able to understand the meaning of words and true enlightenment. If we dispense with finite enlightenment, we cannot conceive of true enlightenment.

(1.) First, finite enlightenment may be viewed in three ways always inseparable from it.

(*a.*) Sensation. When the unenlightened mind is excited we call it sensation. When there is enlightenment there is no excitement; if there is excitement there is pain, as effect follows cause.

(*b.*) Consciousness. This occurs when following any excitement one becomes conscious of something. Without sensation there is no consciousness.

(*c.*) Perception. This is formed when following consciousness the external becomes real. Without consciousness there are no perceptions of outside objects.

Since there is an objective world, there arise again six aspects of it according to another classification, viz:—

(*a.*) Consciousness, which arises from outward objects which the mind distinguishes between one and another—between what it likes and what it dislikes.

(*b.*) Emotion. This follows consciousness and produces joy and sorrow, These false ideas arise from constant partial enlightenment.

(*c.*) Attention. This follows emotion, reaching after everything, seizing on joy and sorrow and cleaving to them with the whole mind.

(*d.*) Conception. This follows perception, distinguishing it by giving it a name.

(*e.*) Will. This follows the giving of names to thigs in all sorts of action.

(*f.*) Discrimination. This is the result of different action and is inevitable. We should know that uninleghtenment can produce all kinds of false methods, because they are within the state of unenlightenment.

(*2.*) Next, infinite enlightenment and finite enlightenment may be viewed together in two ways, viz., where they are the same and where they are different.

(*a.*) As to where they are the same. Take for example the various kinds of pottery : they are all made of one clay. In the same way finite enlightenments are manifestations of the One True Form, and the Sutras according to this doctrine say that all things are eternal and divine. Perfect Enlightenment cannot be cultivated or made, can never be added to and has no form which can be seen. That which has form to be seen accompanies useful transformations. It is not the nature of real Wisdom, for this Wisdom is invisible.

(*b.*) As to where enlightenment and unenlightenment differ, it is like speaking of the different kinds of pots made. Infinite enlightenment and finite enlightenment differ according to their useful transformations, and the infinite nature appears different in the transformations,

(3.) Next, the finite forces which control human nature, such as the changes of mind and consciousness, arise from ignorance and unenlightenment. They may be seen manifested in our feelings and spoken of as mental powers. These mental powers have five names. One is the faculty exercised when in the midst of ignorance finite consciousness begins. The second is the faculty used when the mind takes note of something. The third is the faculty used when all phenomena are put in the objective. Just as outward things are reflected in a mirror, so does this faculty reflect what the five senses show instantaneously at all times. The fourth is the faculty used when distinguishing between the pure and impure. The fifth is the faculty used when it reflects impressions from one object to the other incessantly. It retains the past infinite manifestations of one's own existence with all their good and evil; it ripens into the knowledge of the causes of present and future joy and sorrow which are the unfailing results of our deeds; it is able to call up the past, lay it instantly before our mind and to call up our finite knowledge of the future. Therefore the phenomena of the three worlds (of desire, of form and of no-form) are mind-made. Without mind, then, there is practically no objective existence. Thus all existence arises from imperfect notions of our mind. All differences are differences of the mind. But the mind cannot see itself, for it has no form. We should know that all phenomena are created by the imperfect notions of the finite mind, therefore all existence is like a reflection in a mirror, without substance, only a phantom of the mind. When the finite mind acts, then all kinds of things arise; when the finite mind ceases to act, then all kinds of things cease.

Next, the faculty of thought. This comes out of the fifth as above. In common men this is very strong. The consciousness of self and of environment and all the imperfect ideas arising from these, trying to distinguish between all the objects of the senses, is called thought, and is also called the independent faculty, as well as the faculty of distinguishing things. This increases with the senses, with desires, and with their sorrows.

(4,) As to the origin of imperfect knowledge working in the finite, common men cannot understand this; nor can the wisdom of the two lower schools understand it; only the Pusas, when they begin to get right faith, and when they can examine things properly and test the nature of the True Form, can understand it. Spiritual men can get a small insight into this; even the Pusas when they have attained to their perfect state cannot understand the whole of it. Only Buddha understands all. The mind from the beginning is of a pure nature, but since there is the finite aspect of it which is sullied by finite views, there is the sullied aspect of it. Although there is this defilement, yet the original pure nature is eternally unchanged. This mystery only Buddha understands.

When we speak of the original nature of the mind, eternally without thought, we call it eternally unchanged. As the human mind originally does not know the Archetype (the Absolute Reality) the mind does not correspond with the outward universe. Then thought suddenly begins and is called the finite thought.

Confusion from correspondence with the objective. One can be delivered from this confusion by the two lower schools and be kept far from it in the station of full faith of the great school. Confusion arises through feeling corresponding with the objective. One can gradually avoid this by the cultivation of the means of deliverance in the full faith of the great school; by the cultivation to the First station in the pure state of the mind, all the confusion will be gone. (To understand these and the stations below, see *Guide to Buddhahood.*)

Confusion through knowledge of differences by correspondence with the objective. By means of the second stage of separateness from the world and by means of deliverance in the Seventh station, confusion will be gone.

Confusion through objective forms not corresponding with one another. By means of the Eighth station of freedom from form (or the immoveable) all the confusion will be gone.

Confusion through subjective perception not corresponding with the objective. By means of the Ninth station, when the mind is free (in holy wisdom) the confusion can be got rid of.

Confusion through subjective sensation not corresponding with the objective. By means of the complete ten stations of the Pusas one may enter the state of Ju Lai, Buddhahood, and be delivered from this last of the confusions. As the finite mind does not comprehend the universal Archetype, it begins by the correspondence of faith to examine into things and to rid itself of confusion. In its progress towards purity of mind, it step by step gets rid of confusion and when it arrives at the state of Ju Lai, it is able to be free from it altogether.

The meaning of correspondence is that the finite mind's ideas of the universal True Form differ according to its stages of confusion or enlightenment, and that the perfected finite knowledge and the outside universe are exactly the same. The meaning of want of correspondence is that the finite mind is unenlightened and has never known these differences, and that its knowledge and the outside universe are not the same.

Again the confused mind is a hindrance to thought and darkens the original wisdom of the True Form. Ignorance is called the hindrance of wisdom, and darkens the natural wisdom of the world. What does this mean? It means that, owing to the confused mind, its perceptions, its objects, and thoughts are not in accordance with the eternal nature. It means that owing to the true universal True Form being eternally at rest, without being finite or temporary, ignorance and unenlightenment differ from the eternal, therefore they are unable to follow the perfect wisdom of all the universe.

(5.) Next the finite state. This is of two kinds. First, the rough ordinary state when it corresponds with the finite mind. Second, the fine extraordinary state when it does not correspond with the finite mind. There is also the lowest of the ordinary, such as the state of common men, and the highest of the ordinary. There is, too, the lowest of the extraordinary such as the state of the Pusas; and the highest of the extraordinary, such as the state of Buddha. These two kinds of the finite state arise from the different extent of the influence of ignorance. As to cause and effect, the cause is unenlightenment, the effect is the manufacture of a false imperfect world. If the cause is removed, then the effect is removed. If the imperfect cause ceases, then the imperfect mind which does not correspond with the real universe also ceases. If the result ceases to be erroneous, then the mind which corresponds with the real universe also ceases to be erroneous.

QUESTION 4.—If the finite mind ceases, how can there be continuation? If there be continuation, how then do you speak of finally ceasing altogether?

ANSWER.—What is destroyed is only the finite state of the mind, not the mind's being, just as wind in relation to water is a moving power. If there be no water the effect of the wind is not apparent; there is nothing to show it. If the water remains, the state of the wind is made apparent; only when the wind ceases does the moving of the water cease. It is not the water that ceases to exist. So ignorance in relation to the True real nature is made apparent.

If there were no True Real nature of the mind, then all existence would not exist; there would be nothing to show it. If the True Real Nature of the mind remains, then finite mind continues. Only when the madness of finite mind ceases will the finite mind cease. It is not the wisdom of the True Reality that ceases.

(6.) Influences.—There are four influences—the confused and the pure—incessantly at work. The first is a pure influence called the True Real One. The second is the cause of all confusion, called ignorance. The third is the confused mind, called sensation. The fourth is the false world as known to the senses and called the objective.

Influences may be thus illustrated. Clothes have no scent, but if any one smoked them with incense, the clothes would then be perfumed like the incense. So it is with influences. The True Reality is pure and has really no confusion colouring it, but ignorance in man colours his views so that there is a confused state. The confusion caused by ignorance has really no true purity, but the True Reality influences the mind so that there is an effort after the true purity.

(*a.*) How is it that confused influences are acting incessantly? It is in relation to the True Reality that there is ignorance as a cause of the confusion. This ignorance colours the True Reality in the finite mind. As there is an influence at work, there arise false imperfect ideas, and these colour the True Reality again so that one does not understand it. Unenlightenment then arises bringing a new world of false conceptions on account of this result. These false ideas in turn colour other false conceptions again, causing the mind to be fixed on these and to desire to do all sorts of things, incurring thus all kinds of trouble of both mind and body.

a.a. The influences of the false objective world are of two kinds, viz: those which arise from increased thought, and those which arise from increased action.

bb. The influences of the false imperfection of faculties are of two kinds, viz: those which arise voluntarily from faculties producing the highest saints of the Lower school (the Hinayana) the highest saints (I. e. P'itsz Buddhas,) [See *Guide to Buddhahood*] of the Middle School and the highest saints but one (the Pusas) of the advanced school (the Mahayana) causing them to suffer the sorrows of life and change; and those which arise involuntarily from faculties producing ordinary men and causing them to suffer the sorrows of successive transmigrations.

c.c. The influences of ignorance are of two kinds, first, those which arise from the very root of things—intuition—which give rise to imperfect sensation, and second, those which arise from senses and desires and which give rise to imperfect impressions.

(*b.*) How is it that pure influences are acting incessantly? It is because there is a True Reality able to influence the ignorant, a power at work causing man's misguided mind to dislike the sorrows of transmigration and to seek the joys of divine rest (nirvana). As this ignorant mind is moved to dislike transmigration and love nirvana, this fact influences the finite mind to believe that its nature is finite and to know that its finite mind is full of false ideas, and further, that there is no true objective world before men and that therefore they are to cultivate some way of deliverance. As from the True Reality man knows that there is no objective world, then the various means of following and obeying this True Reality arise spontaneously (without thought and without action) and when influenced by this power for a long time, ignorance disappears. As ignorance disappears, then false ideas cease to arise. As these false ideas do not arise the former objective world also ends. As the forces cease to exist, then the false powers of the finite mind cease to exist, and this is called nirvana, when the natural forces of the True Reality alone work.

a.a. The influence of the imperfect mind is of two kinds, viz: that which arises from positiveness and literalness, as in common men and in those of the two lower schools, causing them to dislike the rounds of transmigration and according to their strength to gradually move towards the unsurpassed way of Buddhism; and that which arises from the five faculties of the mind where the Pusas start to cultivate the True Reality to reach nirvana quickly.

b.b. The influence of the True Reality which is of two kinds, viz: that which arises from subjective influences of the True Reality element itself, and that which arises from outward conditions.

a.a. The influence of the True Reality itself is from eternal ages, having infinite resources and being also complete with benefits beyond all thought. It is also the underlying nature of all phenomena.

On account of this two-fold aspect the power of these influences is unceasing, causing all men to dislike the sorrows of transmigration and seek the joys of nirvana, believing that in their own persons there is the power of the True Reality and that therefore they have a mind to cultivate it.

Question 5.—If this be so, that all living beings have the True Reality in them and that all will be equally influenced, why should there be the infinite distinction of believing and unbelieving, some first and others later? Should not all at the same time know the power of the True Reality, causing them to diligently cultivate the means of deliverance and enabling all to enter nirvana?

Answer.—The True Reality is originally only one, but the degrees of ignorance are infinite, therefore the natures of men differ in character accordingly. There are unruly thoughts more numerous than the sands of the Ganges, some arising from ignorant conceptions and others arising from ignorance of senses and desires. Thus all kinds of wild thoughts arise from ignorance and have first and last infinite differences which Ju Lai alone knows.

Again in the method of all the Buddhas there are means of utilising their forces. The nature and the means must be at work to be complete. Just as wood, though it has fire latent in it (this fire being the real force) cannot burn unless men know this and use means to call it forth, so with men, although there is the power of the influence of the True Reality in them, if it does not meet with the noble forces of the Buddhas and Pusas as a means to call it forth, there would be no means of preventing wild thoughts and of entering nirvana. And although there would be the force of outward conditions, yet without the force of the pure Reality there would not be the power of this Real influence and one could never discard the sorrows of transmigration and seek the joys of nirvana.

If the forces and the means of utilizing them are complete, such as the force of the influences of the True Reality and also of the loving vows of the Buddhas and of the Pusas to save the world, there arises a dislike to sorrow and a belief in nirvana and the cultivation of a good character. When the good character is attained, such people find the Buddhas and Pusas teaching them directly the benefits and the joys of the doctrine and they are able to enter into the way of nirvana.

b.b. The influence of outward conditions. This is the power of outward forces and these outward conditions are incalculable. We indicate two kinds, viz: those of different methods and those of the same spirit.

a.a.a. As to the influences of different methods, they are those which operate when men follow the Buddhas and the Pusas from the beginning of their desire to seek truth till they themselves become Buddhas, and which influence them all through their course, be it in what they see or think, whether through their own family, parents or relatives, or through servants, or dear friends, or through enemies, or by means of the four attractions (such as those caused by alms, kind words, help and sharing in toil) even including all sorts of incalculable means, in order to set in action the power of the loving influences of the Buddhas and Pusas, so as to induce all beings to increase in goodness and benefit by what they see or hear. These means are also of two kinds, viz. the direct, which enables one to get saved quickly, and the indirect, which enables one to get saved after a longer time. The direct and indirect means are again of two kinds, viz. the progressive practice and the final attainment.

b.b.b. As to influences of the same spirit, all the Buddhas and Pusas (who are only one stage lower than the Buddhas) desire to deliver all men from sorrow, and these spirits influence men constantly without ceasing and they are of the same nature and wisdom and power, therefore manifest the same spirit in all their experience. This is experienced when men in their ecstasy are able to see the Buddhas.

c.c. The difference between the influences of the True Form is of two kinds. The first is the uncorresponding. It is that of the common man or of the two lower schools and first stages of the great school of the Pusas. These are influenced by their consciousness and impression, but are able to improve by means of the power of faith. They have not attained to that correspondence of mind with the Absolute whereby they are one with the nature of the True Form, and have not attained that experience which is natural and corresponding to the work of the Absolute.

The second is the corresponding. It is that of the Spiritual Buddhas who have attained to the state when their mind is not different from that of the True Form, but corresponding to the nature and work of all the Buddhas. In this state men are able to act naturally by means of the power of the Absolute Spirituality, and by the influence of the Absolute to put an end to ignorance.

(*c*.) Next note the confused state.

The influence of this confused state has been going on from eternity without ceasing, but when one reaches the state of Buddhahood this ceases. But the influence of the pure state has no end ; it has for ever a future! It is the influence of the Absolute Reality. The confused idea is ended and the spiritual is manifested in the influence it exerts on work and has no end.

(7.) As to the nature and state of the Absolute, that of all common men, that of the lower school, (the Traditional), that of the middle school, that of the Pusas and that of the Buddhas are without a difference, only having more or less of it. It is neither that which had an origin some time, nor that which will end at some time; it is really eternal. In its nature it is always full of all possibitities, and is described as of great light and wisdom, giving light to all things, real and knowing. Its true nature is that of a pure mind, eternally joyful, the true soul of things, pure, quiet, unchanged, therefore free with fulness of virtues and attributes of Buddha more numerous than the sands of the Ganges, divine, unending, unchanged and unspeakable. Most complete, without lacking anything, it is called the treasury or storehouse or womb of Ju Lai, and also the spiritual body of Ju Lai.

QUESTION 6.—Now you have said above that the nature of the Absolute is the same in all beings and is apart from all forms, how is it that you speak of its nature as having all these different possibilities?

ANSWER.—Although real and possessing these possibilities, yet they are not different qualities ; they are of one kind only, one Absolute Reality ; there is a likeness in all the different manifestations, therefore they cannot be different. Again, how do we say that there is a difference? It is in relation to consciousness and the finite that this difference appears. And how does it appear? As regards the origin of all things there is but One Mind, not an unenlightened Mind conjecturing at things, for in the finite there are imperfect ideas. The unenlightened mind begins to think of the world around and this we call ignorance. If this finite thought conjecturing at things had not arisen, there would have been great wisdom and light. When the human mind begins to see that there exists the unseen beyond where the mind nature is independent of this seeing, then it finds that this unseen shines throughout the universe. If the mind is excited or prejudiced, the knowledge is not true knowledge. When it has not found its true nature, it is not eternal, not joyful, not the true soul of things, not pure, but is busy and decaying and therefore not free and thus full of confusion more numerous than the sands of the Ganges. On the other hand, if the mind is not excited or prejudiced by imperfect ideas, all sorts of pure possibilities more numerous than the sands of the Ganges are open to it. If in the human mind there arises an idea to be followed, it is because there is something lacking in the mind. Thus the incalculable possibilities of the pure Absolute Nature is that of the One Mind. There is no need to think out any new idea; it is complete and is called the divine state, the treasury or storehouse or womb of Ju Lai.

(8.) As to the work of the True Form—it is that which is in all the Buddhas and Ju Lai from that first moment of great love and desire to cultivate their own salvation and then to save others, to the time of their great vow to save all beings throughout all future endless kalpas. They regard all living beings as their own selves though they are not the same in form, for in reality all living beings and themselves are manifestations of the

Absolute Reality without any difference; then with the aid of this great wisdom of the True Form they put an end to ignorance, they see the divine and there arise naturally all sorts of unimaginable service like that of the Absolute Reality reaching everywhere. Yet these beings are not ordinary forms, for the Buddhas and Ju Lai are perfect embodiments of the divine. The chief thought is that they are not the ordinary ideas of the world; they are not ordinary workers, but such workers as influence or inspire people in their experiences, hence we say they are the work of the True Form.

(*a.*) This spiritual work of the True Form is of two kinds. The first is dependent on the senses (positive and literal) and on what the mind of the ordinary man and those of the two lower schools understand by them, hence this kind is called the common stage, as these people do not know that their work is the manifestation of their sensation, so regard it outwardly by colour and size, but do not fully know.

(*b.*) The second is dependent on the faculties. It is what all the Pusas from the time they reach the first station till they reach the highest station have experienced, and is called the inspired stage (Pao Shen.) This stage has incalculable manifestions; these manifestions have incalculable states and these states have incalculable blessings.

The results of this stage have also all kinds of incalculable glories according to their manifestations. They are endless and infinite, without measure, ever present in their reactions, indestructible and never lost. These blessings are the results of the perfect influences of the six means of salvation (Paramita) and of the transcendent influences of the Absolute Reality. Thus the Pusas are full of immeasurable joy, hence they are called the inspired spirits.

(*c.*) As to what common men see, it is only the rough outline. These men according to their observations see all sorts of different living creatures in the six kinds of beings (gods, men, ashuras, devils, hungry ghosts, beasts); they have not attained the state of joy, hence they are called common spirits.

(*d*) As to what the Pusas know from the beginning of their free ideas, and what begins to appear to them by full faith in the Absolute Reality, they know some of its characteristics and glory that they are ever present, immeasurable, only manifest in the mind, and inseparable from the Absolute Reality. But these Pusas still have some imperfect notions remaining, as they have not reached the full Divine State. If they reach a purer state of mind and if they progress till they have reached the utmost state, the inspired is seen to perfection.

(*e*) When they pass beyond the sense and faculties, there is no visible state, for the divine soul of all the Buddhas has no outward form by which they are to be seen.

QUESTION 7.—If the divine spirit of all the Buddhas is separated from form, how can it manifest any forms?

ANSWER.—This Divine Soul is the essence of all form, therefore it can manifest itself in form. This is why we say mind and matter are eternally the same. As the essence of matter is wisdom, the essence of matter is without form and is called the embodiment of wisdom. As the manifested essence of wisdom is matter, it is called the all-pervading embodiment of wisdom. The unmanifested matter is without magnitude; according to the will it can show itself throughout all the universe as the immeasurable Pusas, immeasurable inspired spirits, immeasurable glories, all different without magnitude and without interference with one another. This is what ordinary senses cannot comprehend, as it is the work of the True Form (Absolute Reality).

(9.) Now we show how to proceed from the finite to the infinite. This is called analysing all experience matter to mind. In all the six objects of sense there does not exist false conjectures as men's thoughts are. As the mind has no form we seek for it at all points of space in vain. Just as a man having lost his way calls the east, west, although the east and west have not really changed, so is mankind lost in ignorance calling the mind of the universe his thoughts! But the Mind is what it ever was, all unchanged by men's thought. When men consider and realise that the Absolute Mind has no need of thoughts like men, they are then following the right way to reach the Infinite.

B.—The rectification of erroneous conceptions. All kinds of erroneous conceptions arise from our own conceptions of things. If we could put away these personal conceptions, there would then be no false ones. These personal conceptions are of two kinds, viz: false conceptions of the person (selfish anthropology) as the self, and false conceptions of that which regards as the self.

1. That which regards personal being as self.

According to common language it is of five kinds.

a. Hearing the Sutras saying that the eternal nature of Ju Lai is in the end only vacuity like space, some men, not knowing that this expression was used in order to destroy belief in phenomena as real, say that Space or Emptiness itself is Ju Lai. How is this to be rectified? Men are to understand that space is nothing. It has no existence and is not a reality. It is a term in opposition to reality. We only say this or that is visible in order that we might distinguish between things. All phenomena are originally in the Mind and have really no outward form, therefore as there is no form it is a mistake to think there is anything there. All phenomena only arise from false notions of the Mind. If the Mind is independent of these false ideas, then all phenomena disappear. This is called the true glorious nature and wisdom of Ju Lai and not mere empty space.

b. Hearing the Sutras saying that the nature of all things in the world is unreal, even the final nature of nirvana and of the True Form (the Absolute Reality) therefore they are also intangible and eternally independent of all forms, some men, not knowing that it was for the purpose of destroying belief in phenomena that these expressions were used, say the nature of the Absolute Reality and nirvana is nothing but unreality. How is this to be rectified? They are to understand that the divine nature of the Absolute Reality is not unreal. It is full of infinite possibilities.

c. Hearing the Sutras saying that the treasures of Ju Lai are eternally fixed without addition or substraction and are potentially full of all possibilities, some men, not understanding it, say the treasures of Ju Lai contain both the distinctions of mind and matter. How is this to be rectified? According to the Absolute Reality there is no distinction between mind and matter, it is on account of the defilement of the finite in the round of life and death that these distinctions appear.

d. Hearing the Sutras saying that all the defilements of life and death exist because they are in the treasury of Ju Lai, as nothing is independent of the Absolute Reality, some men not understanding it say the attributes of Ju Lai originally contain everything that there is in the world pertaining to life and death. How is this to be rectified? As the attributes of Ju Lai from eternity only contain pure possibilities more numerous than the sands of the Ganges, they are not independent of the Absolute Reality. They never fail and are not different from the Absolute Reality. As to the defilements of the world, they are all false; they have no reality behind them. From eternity they have had nothing in them corresponding to Ju Lai. If there had been defilement in the nature of Ju Lai's attributes, to get rid of defilement by causing men to unite with Ju Lai would be an absurdity.

e. Hearing the Sutras saying that life and death depend on the treasures of Ju Lai and that nirvana also depends on the treasures of Ju Lai, some men not understanding it say that all beings have a beginning and as they have a beginning they then say that the joys of nirvana which Ju Lai has obtained have an end when he comes again incarnate. How is this to be rectified? As the treasures of Ju Lai are without a beginning, so is the state of ignorance without a beginning. If it be said that beyond the three worlds—earth, heaven and hell, or form, desire, and no-form—there are other beings, this is but the talk of Non-Buddhist Scriptures. Moreover as the treasures of Ju Lai are without an end, so is nirvana. which all the Buddhas obtain, without end.

2. To meet the intelligent of the two lower schools, Ju Lai only spoke to them of the Absolute as not like men (not anthropology). As he had not spoken fully to them of the temporary nature of experience, they feared the rounds of life and death and sought a false nirvana. How is this to be rectified? As the nature behind all experience has no beginning, so it has no end—this is the true nirvana.

3. Finally, to leave false conceptions, one should know that purity and defilement are both relative terms and have no independent existence. Although all things from eternity are neither matter nor mind, neither infinite wisdom nor finite knowledge, neither existing nor non-existing, but are after all inexpressible, we nevertheless use

words, yet should know that Ju Lai's skilful use of words to lead men aright lay in this—to get men to cease conjecturing and to return to the Absolute Reality, for the best human thought of all things is only temporary and is not Absolute truth.

C.—Different steps of progress. These are the paths which all the Buddhas have passed through and the goals reached by the Pusas when they have made up their minds to practice religion. Briefly speaking, religious growth or progress involves having three things: first, growth of perfect faith, second, growth in intelligent practice, third, growth in attainments.

1. The progress of perfect faith. It depends on the kind of man and the kind of character he has, whether he gets a perfect faith worthy of progress. This again depends on uncertainty of character whether tending to good or evil. If influenced by goodness, believing that good and evil have their respective recompense, if able to abound in all sorts of good works, if tired with the sorrows of life and death. if desiring to obtain the highest wisdom by meeting all the Buddhas and by worshipping and supporting them in person and practising faith long under all conditions, then faith is perfect and the Buddhas and Pusas teach such how to progress. Some moved by great pity are able to progress of themselves, others on seeing the right doctrine about to be attacked are moved to defend it. Such persons are able to progress. Thus when faith is perfect and the religious aim is fixed, they enter the ranks of the upright and true fixed ones, they never go back and are reckoned among the seed of the children of Ju Lai, being one with the right eternal Cause of things.

a. If the root of goodness in man be small, in the long run worldly affairs are like thick weeds choking it. Although these people should begin worshipping and supporting the Buddhas, they only become the seed to be born in a better state among men or in the abode of the lower gods, or may become the seed of the two lower schools of Buddhism or may cultivate the great school. But goodness is uncertain—it may have taken root or may not. Or if men serve the Buddhas, though they have not served them very long, yet on account of going through special circumstances they also may strike root and grow. This will only be if they regard the Buddhas in a special manner, or, if they also learn from the followers of the two lower schools, they also may grow. On account of following the example of others they also may grow. Those progressing for these latter reasons are all uncertain. When they meet adverse circumstances they fall back from the highest Faith to the two lower ones.

b. Next, what is the progress of perfect faith? Briefly speaking it is three-fold. First, it is upright having right thoughts of the eternal. Second, it is profound, rejoicing to study everything that is good and to practise it. Third, it is greatly pitiful, anxious to deliver all living beings from their sorrow.

QUESTION 8.—Formerly you said that all the universe was but one state and that the Natures of the Gods were not different from that of men, so how is it that it is not only by the study of the Eternal and by practice of all kinds of goodness that one reaches that state?

ANSWER.—Man's nature is like a great precious stone. It is bright and pure, but there is the dross of the quarry on it. If men think only of its precious nature and do not use various means to cleanse it, it will never be pure. Thus is it with mankind. The nature of the eternal in them is absolute purity but it is defiled with infinite dross. If men only think of the eternal and do not use various means to improve their nature they also will never get pure, because there is infinite dross pervading everything. The practice of all sorts of good is in order to purge away the dross. If men practise all sorts of good, they will naturally fall in with the eternal way.

c. Briefly speaking, the means are of four kinds.

(1.) Cultivate the root of things, by looking on the true nature of all things as eternal, without beginning, independent of man's conception of things and not permanent in temporary life, by looking on all things linked together by a never failing law of deeds and their consequences, by nourishing a great pity and cultivating virtue joyfully, by seeking to save all men, not resting in the nirvana of the two lower schools, as that which does nothing for the Eternal Archetype never rests.

(2.) Cease from evil. It is by contrition and repentance that one is enabled to cease from all evil and prevent its increase. As one follows the eternal nature he departs from all evil.

(3.) Grow in goodness. It is by diligently honouring and supporting the Three Precious Ones, praising them, rejoicing in their good deeds and by seeking instructions of the Enlightened. As there is love and respect for the holy character of the Three Precious Ones, faith grows and one desires to get the first doctrine.

Besides the influence of God, there is that of His law throughout the universe, and that of the priesthood, the teachers of this law, by which one is able to remove the hindrances to goodness and be firmly rooted in it, for one follows and obeys eternal law and leaves mad hindrances far behind.

(4.) Seek the Eternal's wish. It is an ever growing desire to save all living beings without exception, so that all may reach the Supreme Nirvana (Rest) of the Higher Faith where one follows and obeys the nature of the

Eternal for ever. The Eternal nature is vast and pervading all living beings without distinction of this, that, or the other and is the final rest of all.

d. As an intelligent devout man (Pusa) thus progresses in religion, he begins to comprehend a little of the Eternal state. As he comprehends the Eternal he discovers that the Eternal has made eight kinds of sacrifices for men. He descends from his heaven of ease (the Tow Swai). He becomes incarnate and mingles with his less fortunate fellow-beings. He grows in the womb of obscurity. He becomes well-known. He sacrifices all other interests, even his home, and becomes a priest devoted to the Eternal. He discovers true religion. He preaches the law of the Eternal. He enters the true Nirvana of perfect peace.

But this intelligent devout man (Pusa) is not called the divine eternal embodiment. As in the innumerable ages of the past there still remain some deeds which he has not been able to free entirely from defilement, so there are sufferings corresponding to them in his circumstances, but he is not bound by these imperfections any longer.

Since he is free by the power of the Great Eternal to save men, the Sutra says if we speak of the Pusa going down to some evil place he is not really degraded thereby. It is only in the beginning that it appears so and therefore he descends to strengthen some who are hesitating in fear.

f. Moreover the Pusa from the beginning of his perfect faith is far from having any weakness and never has any fear of falling back to the state of the two lower schools. Even if he hear that nirvana cannot be obtained till after patient toil through troubles lasting for immeasurable and endless kalpas of longest durations, still he faints not, as by faith he knows that behind all existence there is naturally the Supreme Nirvana (Rest).

2. Growth in intelligent practice. One must know that there must be growth. When the Pusas who from the first follow the correct faith are about to complete the first term of long kalpas, they then fully comprehend the Eternal. It is in a state of complete independence of all form and they practice those divine exercises by means of which they pass into the Supreme Nirvana. As they learn that the Eternal has no selfishness, they then follow obediently the practice of the divine (Paramita) kinds of charity. As they learn that the Eternal is undefiled, free from the sins arising from the longings of the five senses, they then follow obediently the practice of the divine (Paramita) perseverance. As they learn that the Eternal is ever clear, without confusion, they then follow obediently the practice of the divine (Paramita) unchangeableness.

As they learn that the Eternal is all intelligence, free from ignorance, they then follow obediently the practice of the divine (Paramita) wisdom.

3. Growth in attainments. This covers the ground from the beginning of the holy pure state up to the highest attainments of Pusaship. What attainments are these? They are those of the Eternal. According to the perception of the senses this would be called the objective world, but in our present attainment there is nothing outward but the eternal wisdom which is called the Divine body.

a. These Pusas in an instant are able to reach all space throughout all the universe, adoring all the enlightened gods (Buddhas) and requesting them to explain the Eternal law for the sole purpose of teaching and benefiting all living beings, so as to get the spirit of the law and not mere fine words. These Pusas sometimes hurry over various stages of progress so as to get right enlightenment speedily in order to help the weak, sometimes after a term of countless long kalpas they may become Buddhas in order to encourage the weary ones, and thus show by countless ways how to attain Buddhaship. In reality as the root of the nature of the seed of Pusaship is the same, the growth is the same and the attainment is the same viz: through the Eternal way. There is no such thing as omitting any term, as all the Pusas must go through the three terms; though they follow different ways with different men. As men's nature, desires, and dispositions are different, the Pusas show different methods for their salvation.

b. Here the growth of this state of Pusa is threefold and is very necessary. The first is that of the true soul which in no way differs from the Eternal. The second is that of the different means employed to meet the needs of all beings. The third is that of his conceptions of things where still linger a few false notions disturbing him.

c. Then comes the Pusas' perfection in all virtues at the head of the world of form, showing themselves as the greatest of mortals. In a moment they correspond exactly to the eternal wisdom, and all ignorance being entirely gone, this correspondence is called the root seed of all wisdom. These Pusas naturally possess powers beyond all thought, able to manifest themselves throughout all points of space for the good of all beings.

QUESTION 9.—As space is infinite, worlds are infinite. As worlds are infinite, living beings are infinite. As living beings are infinite, the differences of thought in them are infinite and in such a state their respective magnitudes cannot be determined, none can know or explain them. If ignorance is removed then no vain guesses will exist. How can we understand that which is called the seed of wisdom?

ANSWER.—All the universe originally was only *One Soul* needing not to conjecture at things. As living beings only imperfectly see the world outside them, their minds are limited and they begin to make idle conjectures different from the reality thus preventing a right understanding of things. All the Buddhas and Ju Lai are independent of the senses and omniscient. The real soul is the nature of all things. This soul shines forth on all minds. It has great wisdom in innumerable ways according to the different needs of men so as to instruct them in all kinds of ways. On this account it has been named the seed of all wisdom.

QUESTION 10.—If the Buddhas have a natural power to manifest themselves everywhere for the good of all living beings, and if all beings see their manifested bodies, then men observe their various modifications and if they hear their words which are good, how do you say that most people cannot see them?

ANSWER.—The divine nature of the Buddhas and of Ju Lai is one pervading all space without any effort of the mind, therefore we say it is natural yet depending on men for its manifestation. The soul of living beings is just like a mirror. If it is not clear it cannot reflect. So if the soul of living beings is not pure, the divine nature cannot be properly reflected.

CHAPTER IV.

The Practice of the Mahayana Faith.

Having illustrated the principles we now discuss the practice of them. This is on account of those who have not entered the ranks of the upright ones and so we explain the practice of Faith. What faith? what practice? Briefly speaking, faith is of four kinds. First, belief in the root of all things, that is, rejoicing to think of the Absolute Reality (True Form). Second, belief in the infinite merits of Divinity (Buddhahood) ever thinking of it, drawing near to it, supporting and adoring it, growing in goodness and seeking all wisdom from it. Third, belief in the great benefit of the law, always thinking how to practise all the different means of salvation. Fourth, belief in the priesthood's ability to cultivate the right doctrine; having themselves found good, they help others to obtain it; ever rejoicing to approach all the Pusas and seeking to learn and practise the truth as it is in the Eternal.

To realize the faith, practice consists of *five stages*. These five are:

1—The stage of charity.

2—The stage of holiness.

3—The stage of enduring wrong.

4—The stage of perseverance.

5—The stage of preventing vain thoughts and the practice of reflection.

A.—How to practise the state of charity. If one sees any coming to beg in their need, money should be given them according to one's ability in order to prevent covetousness in oneself and to make the poor glad. If one sees men in trouble, fear and danger, the fear should be relieved according to one's power. If men come to inquire about religion, one should explain the various means according to one's ability. In all things one should not seek the honours of fame or wealth, but, simply feeling that having received benefit oneself, one should impart the same benefit to others so that they may return to true wisdom.

B.—How to practise the state of holiness. This is to observe the *Ten commandments.*

1—Thou shalt not kill anything.
2—Thou shalt not steal.
3—Thou shalt not commit adultery.
4—Thou shalt not be doublefaced.
5—Thou shalt not curse.
6—Thou shalt not lie.
7—Thou shalt not speak vanity.
8—Thou shalt keep far from coveting.
9—Thou shalt not insult, deceive, flatter or trick.
10—Thou shalt be free from anger and heresy.

As for the priests, in order to overcome the temptations of the world they should keep far from the stir of the world and ever live in quietness, cultivating few desires and satisfaction with their lot, while mortifications should take place after committing the smallest sin. Their hearts must be moved with fear and most sincere repentance and in no way must they regard the prohibitions of Ju Lai lightly. They should also guard against appearances of evil, lest men should commit the sin of speaking evil against the priests.

C.—How to practise the state of bearing the cross (enduring wrong). This is what is called the duty of enduring the aspersions of others without a feeling of revenge through the eight storms of life. That is, to be the same in prosperity, in adversity, in honour and dishonour, in good and evil report, in trouble and in joy.

D.—How to practise the state of perseverance. The heart, must be never weary in well doing of all sorts, having a purpose firm and strong, far from any weakness. Thinking of having passed in vain through all the great sorrows of mind and body down through past ages without doing any good, to advance in the scale of being one should diligently practise all sorts of good. Having obtained good oneself one should make this known to others so as to speedily leave all sorrow.

Next, although some men practise faith, yet, as from former generations they had many grave sins and delusions, they are troubled by all sorts of evil spirits, or are bound by all sorts of affairs of the world, or are troubled with sicknesses or with many similar trials; they must therefore have courage and diligence and worship God (Buddha) night and day at all the appointed times, repent with all sincerity, seek light from Buddha, rejoice with others' good so as to return towards true wisdom. This should be done constantly without intermission so as to escape from all delusions and to grow in all goodness.

E.—How to practise the state of checking idle thought and of cultivating sound reflection. To check idle thought is to cease from being misled by impressions and to follow and obey the rules. To reflect is to differentiate between the different laws of temporary existence and to obey the rules of reflection. How are these to be followed? These two states are to be gradually cultivated, not independently, but simultaneously.

1.—As to the practice of checking vain thoughts. it should be done in a quiet place, properly seated and in a proper spirit. It is not the practice of breathing air in a special manner into the body, as is the custom of some religions thinking thereby to get the vital spirit of nature into the body, nor the use of anything that has form or colour, whether of empty space or of the four elements earth, water, fire and wind, or even of the knowledge gained by any experience of the senses, for all kinds of ideas as soon as thought of must be put away, even the idea of banishing them must also be put away. As all existence originally came to be without any idea of its own, it ceases to be also without any idea of its own, any thoughts arising therefore must be from being absolutely passive. Nor must one follow the mind in its excursions to everything outside itself and then chase that thought away. If the mind wanders far away it must be brought back into its proper state. One should know that the proper state is that of the Soul alone without anything outside of it. Again, even this soul has no form and no thought by which we can conceive of it properly.

a.—Having risen from the sitting posture whether in going out or coming in, or in any work, at all times one should think of the means of checking vain thoughts and should examine whether he succeeds in it or whether he follows them. In time one gets perfect in the practice and the mind is at rest. As the mind is at rest it gradually gets courage to proceed; in this way it reaches the peace of the Eternal far beyond all trouble with faith increasing so that it will soon be so perfect as never to fail any more. But doubters, unbelievers, blasphemers, great sinners, those who are conceited, who will not persevere and such-like people cannot obtain this peace of the Eternal.

b.—Note next that by this peace one knows that in the spiritual world the peace of the spiritual bodies of all the Buddhas and of all living bodies are one and the same and is called Divine peace. Know that the root of this peace is in the Eternal. If this is continued there gradually arises in the mind an infinite peace.

C.—If there should be some men without the strength which comes from good deeds who are troubled with evil spirits and the gods and demons of outside religions, appearing sometimes in ugly forms causing fear to them whilst sitting in contemplation; at other times appearing in lovely forms to tempt them, they should think of the *One Eternal Soul*, then these appearances will vanish and give no more trouble. These evil spirits, whether taking the form of the heavenly beings, of Pusas (Earthly Saints) or of Ju Lai, all full of perfection, or using magic formulae, or preaching charity, morality endurance of wrong, perseverance, contemplation, wisdom, or discussing the one unseen reality, the formless reality, the passionless reality, without enmity and without love, without cause and without effect—nothing but pure emptiness—say that this is the true Nirvana! They also teach men how to know the past and to know the future and how to know what is in the mind of others and how to have unfailing gifts of speech, causing men to covet the fame and wealth of this world.

Or again these evil spirits cause men to be frequently violently angry or very happy, without anything to steady them, sometimes to have great compassion, or to be sleepy or ill or to be without perseverance, or they cause men to persevere for a time and then to fall back worse than ever, to lose faith, to have many doubts and fears, or give up their practice of checking vain thoughts and make them follow miscellaneous matters and be chained by the many affairs of the world, so as to give men a certain kind of peace, somewhat similar to the true peace, but which is the product of outside religions and not the true peace of the Eternal.

Or again, these evil spirits cause men for one, two, three, or even seven days to remain in contemplation as if enjoying delicious food; they are most happy in mind and body without any hunger or thirst, or they may be led to eat without any control, sometimes much and sometimes little, so that the countenance changes and exhibits gladness or sorrow accordingly.

As there are such things, religious people should always wisely examine themselves lest their minds should fall into the nets of heresy. They should carefully rectify their thoughts and neither adopt nor be attached to them, but keep themselves far from all delusions.

One should know that the peace of outside religions is of the senses, of the affections to gratify self, desiring the honours of fame and the wealth of the world.

But the true peace is not in the realms of the senses or in possessions and even after contemplation there is neither the feeling of having attained perfection with no further effort nor conceit for what has been accomplished. All trials gradually diminish.

If men do not cultivate this peace there is no other way to get the seed of Ju Lai (the Divine Incarnate Lord).

As the peace of this world mostly arises from the pleasure which is given to the senses, it is bound to the three worlds of form, of desire, and of no-form, like that of the outside religions. Once men leave the guidance of sound wisdom, there arise at once false doctrines.

d. Next note that those who diligently set their minds on securing this peace should in the present generation obtain ten advantages:

(1.) All the Buddhas and Pusas (Saints) throughout all space always protect them.

(2.) None of the evil spirits can cause them any fear.

(3.) They cannot be deceived by any of the 95 kinds of outside religions.

(4.) They are far beyond questioning the deep things of the Buddhist religion, and great sins gradually diminish.

(5.) There is an end to all doubt and all kinds of heresies.

(6.) Faith in the world of Ju Lai grows.

(7.) They leave sorrow far behind in the minds of mortals, while they themselves have no fear.

(8.) Their spirits become gentle and peaceable, they put off pride and conceit and are not troubled by other people's opinions.

(9.) Although they have not obtained full peace at all times and in every place, they are able to lessen their trials and do not covet the world's pleasures.

(10.) When their peace is secured they are unmoved by any seductions of outside attractions.

2.—Now if men practise only contemplation, the mind is damped, or gets weary, and does not rejoice in all goodness but is far from pity, therefore it is necessary to cultivate reasoning or reflection.

a. One should reflect that nothing made throughout the universe can last long; in a moment it may be destroyed.

b. One should reflect that all thought rises and vanishes again like a wave and is therefore a sorrow.

c. One should reflect that all the past is misty like a dream, that all the present is like lightning, that all the future rises suddenly like a cloud in the sky.

d. One should reflect that the bodies of all living beings are unclean, full of all kinds of uncleanness, and therefore not to be rejoiced in.

e. Thus one should reflect that all living beings, from eternity down the ages, being influenced by ignorance, live and die and endure all the great sorrows of mind and body; and reflect on the endless trials of the present and on the immeasurable sorrows of the future which cannot be got rid of and which men are scarcely aware of. When all men's lives are so full of sorrow they are greatly to be pitied.

f. Having thought of these things one should stir oneself up to make a great vow to lead one's own soul to leave the finite and gain the infinite, cultivate every means of grace to deliver all men for ever from their sorrows and obtain the highest joys of nirvana.

g. Having made this great vow one must not give up practising it or be weary in it, but at all times and all places engage in every good that is in one's power.

3. Whilst sitting in meditation one's mind should be bent on checking vain thoughts. At other times one should reflect carefully in regard to everything whether it should or should not be done. Whether walking or resting, lying down or rising up, both reflecting and checking vain thoughts should go together. This is what is meant by the saying that although we practise all these things, our perfection is not really produced by ourselves, but by the nature of the Eternal working through us.

Again thinking of the never-failing law of cause and effect and joy and sorrow as the reward of good and evil, when we think of law we must also think of this goal so difficult to attain.

The practice of checking vain thoughts is to sever the attachments of ordinary men to the world and to put away the fears and weaknesses of the two lower schools of Buddhism.

The practice of reflection is to deliver from the narrow sin of the two lower schools who do not have the vow of great pity for others and who do not keep far from ordinary men who do not practise goodness.

In this way the two methods of reflection and vain thoughts are mutually helpful to one another and inseparable. If both are not practised one cannot then enter on the way of wisdom.

4. Next consider those who begin to learn the five methods of this Chapter and desire to get right faith but are timid and weak. As they live in this world of extreme suffering, they fear they cannot constantly approach God (Buddha) and personally contribute to His service. Thus they fear they cannot attain to this perfect faith and have a mind to renounce their search after it.

These should know that Ju Lai has most excellent means to strengthen their faith. It is by having the mind set only on the things of Buddha and by desiring that one may be born in another world of Buddha and be constantly with Him for ever far from all evil that one may attain this end. As the Sutra says, if a man sets his mind to think only of Amtiabha Buddha who is in the happiest realm of the west (Paradise), and if his good deeds are in the right direction and if he desires to be born in that happy Paradise, he will then be born there, and as he is always in the respence of Buddha he will never fall back.

If we reflect on the eternal nature of Amitabha Buddha and constantly practise this method, one will in the end reach the place of true wisdom.

CHAPTER V.

The Advantages of the Practice of the Mahayana Faith.

Having discussed the practice of these principles, we will now discuss the advantages of practising them. We have already given a general idea of the mysterious resources of the Buddhas of the Mahayana School.

A.—If any one desires to get a right faith in the deep things of Julai, and desires to be far from error which brings religion into disrepute, and to get the Mahayana Faith, he should lay hold of this book, study it and practise it. In the end he will attain to the very highest doctrine.

B.—If a man listens to this doctrine and has neither fear nor weakness, such a man is certain to succeed to the rank of Buddha and to be enrolled as such by all the Buddhas.

C.—If a man should be able to reform all living beings throughout all the systems in the universe, in order to make them good, he would not be equal to a man who for only the time he takes to a meal studies this way of deliverance. The two methods are incomparable.

D.—Next if a man takes this book, studies and practises it only for a day and a night, the blessing received would be incalculable. Even if all the Buddhas of the universe were each to speak of these blessings for incalculably and immeasureably long kalpas, they could not exhaust them, for the blessings of the Eternal Nature are endless and the blessings to this man would be also in like manner boundless.

E.—But if there should be any who speak evil and do not believe in this book, the recompense of their sin will be to suffer immense pain for measureless ages. On this account all men should respectfully believe and not speak evil of it thereby injuring themselves more and more and others too, destroying every hope of deliverance by destroying the Eternal soul of the Three Precious Ones originally in man (the soul of the universe, the body of laws pervading the universe, the body of men teaching these laws) for all the Buddhas (Ju Lai) attain to nirvana by this means and all the Pusas attain Buddha-wisdom by the same practice.

F.—Know that it is by this means that the Pusas of the past obtained pure faith, and that it is by this means that the Pusas of the present obtain pure faith, therefore tt is by this means that the Pusas of the future must iobtain pure faith. Thus all men should diligently study and practise it.

The closing Hymn.

Deep and wide are Buddhist laws.
These in brief I have declared
God-ward are eternal stores,
Blessings give to countless worlds.

THE END.

迴此功德如法性　普利一切衆生界

大乘起信論

明治二十一年三月廿三日　印刷

同　同　三月廿五日　出版

發行者　永田長左衛門

著作者　藤井玄珠

印刷者　林繁次郎

大乘起信論校註

上海
華美書局代印

大乘起信論

馬鳴菩薩造

梁天竺三藏法師眞諦譯

歸命盡十方　最勝業遍知　色無礙自在
救世大悲者　及彼身體相　法性眞如海
無量功德藏　如實修行等　爲欲令衆生
除疑捨邪執　起大乘正信　佛種不斷故

論曰。有法能起摩訶衍信根。是故應說。說有五分。云何爲五。一者因緣分。二者立義分。三者解釋分。四者修行信心分。五者勸修利益分。

Q1. D G
I A B C E F H Q2,

初說因緣分。

問曰。有何因緣而造此論。答曰。是因緣有八種。云何爲八。一者因緣總相。所謂爲令衆生離一切苦得究竟樂。非求世間名利恭敬故。二者爲欲解釋如來根本之義。令諸衆生正解不謬故。三者爲令善根成熟衆生於摩訶衍法堪任不退信心故。四者爲令善根微少衆生修習信心故。五者爲示方便消惡業障善護其心遠離癡慢出邪網故。六者爲示修習止觀對治凡夫二乘心過故。七者爲示專念方便生於佛前必定不退信心故。八者爲示利益勸修行故。有如是等因緣所以造論。問曰。修多羅中具有此法。何須重說。答曰。修多羅中雖有此法。以衆生根行不等受解緣別。所謂

如來在世衆生利根。能說之人色心業勝。圓音一演異類等解則不須論。若如來滅後。或有衆生能以自力廣聞而取解者。或有衆生亦以自力少聞而多解者。或有衆生無自心力因於廣論而得解者。自有衆生復以廣論文多爲煩心樂總持少文而攝多義能取解者。如是此論爲欲總攝如來廣大深法無邊義故。應說此論。

II 已說因緣分。次說立義分。

A 摩訶衍者。總說有二種。云何爲二。一者法。二者義。所言法者謂衆生心。是心則攝一切世間法出世間法。依於此心顯示摩訶衍義。何以故。是心眞

B 如相。卽示摩訶衍體故。是心生滅因緣相。能示摩訶衍自體相用故。所言

1, A III

義者。則有三種。云何爲三。一者體大。謂一切法眞如。平等不增減故。二者相大。謂如來藏具足無量性功德故。三者用大。謂能生一切世間出世間善因果故。一切諸佛本所乘故。一切菩薩皆乘此法到如來地故。

已說立義分次說解釋分。

解釋有三種。云何爲三。一者顯示正義。二者對治邪執。三者分別發趣道相。顯示正義者。依一心法有二種門。云何爲二。一者心眞如門。二者心生滅門。是二種門。皆各總攝一切法。此義云何。以是二門不相離故。

心眞如者。卽是一法界大總相法門體。所謂心性不生不滅。一切諸法唯依妄念而有差別。若離心念則無一切境界之相。是故一切法從本已來。

離言說相。離名字相。離心緣相。畢竟平等。無有變異。不可破壞。唯是一心。故名眞如。以一切言說假名無實。但隨妄念不可得故。言眞如者。亦無有相。謂言說之極。因言遣言。此眞如體。無有可遣。以一切法悉皆眞故。亦無可立。以一切法皆同如故。當知一切法。不可說不可念故。名爲眞如。問曰。若如是義者。諸衆生等云何隨順而能得入。答曰。若知一切法雖說無有能說可說。雖念亦無能念可念。是名隨順。若離於念名爲得入。

復次眞如者。依言說分別有二種義。云何爲二。一者如實空。以能究竟顯實故。二者如實不空。以有自體具足無漏性功德故。所言空者。從本已來一切染法不相應故。謂離一切法差別之相。以無虛妄心念故。當知眞如

a　2,　b

自性。非有相非無相非非有相非非無相。非有無俱相。非一相非異相、非非一相。非非異相。非一異俱相。乃至總說。依一切衆生以有妄心念念分別。皆不相應故說爲空。若離妄心實無可空故。

言所不空者。已顯法體空無妄故。卽是眞心常恒不變淨法滿足則名不空。亦無有相可取。以離念境界唯證相應故。

心生滅者。依如來藏故有生滅心。所謂不生不滅與生滅和合非一非異。名爲阿梨耶識。此識有二種義。能攝一切法生一切法。云何爲二。一者覺義。二者不覺義。

所言覺義者。謂心體離念。離念相者等虛空界無所不偏法界一相。卽是

如來平等法身。依此法身說名本覺。何以故。本覺義者。對始覺義說。以始覺者卽同本覺。始覺義者。依本覺故。而有不覺、依不覺故。說有始覺。

又以覺心源故。名究竟覺。不覺心源故。非究竟覺。此義云何。如凡夫人、覺知前念起惡故。能止後念令其不起。雖復名覺。卽是不覺故。如二乘觀智。初發智菩薩等。覺於念異。念無異相。以捨麤分別執著相故。名相似覺。如法身菩薩等。覺於念住。念無住相。以離分別麤念相故。名隨分覺。如菩薩地盡。滿足方便一念相應、覺心初起。心無初相。以遠離微細念故。得見心性。心卽常住。名究竟覺。是故修多羅說。若有衆生能觀無念者、則爲向佛智故。又心起者。無有初相可知。而言知初相者、卽謂無念。是故一切衆生

不名爲覺。以從本來念念相續未曾離念。故說無始無明。若得無念者。則知心相生住異滅。以無念等故。而實無有始覺之異。以四相俱時而有。皆無自立。本來平等同一覺故。

復次本覺隨染。分別生二種相。與彼本覺不相捨離。云何爲二。一者智淨相。二者不思議業相。智淨相者。謂依法力熏習。如實修行。滿足方便故。破和合識相。滅相續心相。顯現法身。智淳淨故。此義云何。以一切心識之相皆是無明。無明之相。不離覺性。非可壞。非不可壞。如大海水因風波動。水相風相不相捨離。而水非動性。若風止滅。動相則滅。濕性不壞故。如是衆生自性淸淨心。因無明風動。心與無明俱無形相。不相捨離。而心非動性

(b) 若無明滅相續則滅。智性不壞故。不思議業相者。以依智淨相。能作一切勝妙境界。所謂無量功德之相。常無斷絕。隨衆生根自然相應種種而現得利益故。

(2)

(a) 復次覺體相者。有四種大義。與虛空等。猶如淨鏡。云何爲四。一者如實空鏡。遠離一切心境界相。無法可現。非覺照義故。

(b) 二者因熏習鏡。謂如實不空。一切世間境界悉於中現。不出不入不失不壞。常住一心。以一切法卽眞實性故。又一切染法所不能染。智體不動。具足無漏熏衆生故。

(c) 三者法出離鏡。謂不空法。出煩惱礙智礙。離和合相。淳淨明故。

(d) 四者緣熏習鏡。謂依法出離故。徧照衆生之心。令修善根。隨念示現故。

b 所言不覺義者。謂不如實知眞如法一故。不覺心起而有其念。念無自相不離本覺。猶如迷人依方故迷。若離於方則無有迷。衆生亦爾。依覺故迷。若離覺性則無不覺。以有不覺妄想心故。能知名義爲說眞覺。若離不覺之心。則無眞覺自相可說。

(1)

(a) 復次依不覺故生三種相。與彼不覺相應不相離。云何爲三。一者無明業相。以依不覺故心動說名爲業。覺則不動。動則有苦。果不離因故。

(b) 二者能見相。以依動故能見。不動則無見。

(c) 三者境界相。以依能見故境界妄現。離見則無境界。

(d1) 以有境界故復生六種相。云何爲六。一者智相。依於境界心起分別愛與不愛故。

(e2) 二者相續相。依於智故生其苦樂覺心。起念相應不

(f)(g4) 斷故。三者執取相、依於相續緣念境界、住持苦樂。心起著故。四者計名字
(h5) 相。依於妄執分別假名言相故。五者起業相。依於名字尋名取著造種種
(i6) 業故。六者業繫苦相。以依業受報不自在故。當知無明能生一切染法。以
一切染法皆是不覺相故、

(2)(a) 復次覺與不覺有二種相。云何爲二。一者同相。二者異相。言同相者。譬如
種種瓦器皆同微塵性相。如是無漏無明種種業幻、皆同眞如性相。是故
修多羅中。依於此眞如義故。說一切衆生本來常住入於槃涅菩提之法
非可修相。非可作相。畢竟無得、亦無色相可見。而有見色相者。唯是隨染
(b) 業幻所作、非是智色不空之性。以智相無可見故。言異相者。譬如種種瓦

器各各不同。如是無漏無明。隨染幻差別。性染幻差別故。

(3) 復次生滅因緣者。所謂衆生依心意意識轉故。此義云何。以依阿梨耶識說有無明不覺而起能見能現。能取境界。起念相續。故說爲意。此意復有五種名。云何爲五。(a) 一者名爲業識。謂無明力不覺心動故。(b) 二者名爲轉識。依於動心能見相故。(c) 三者名爲現識。所謂能現一切境界。猶如明鏡現於色像。現識亦爾。隨其五塵對至卽現。無有前後。以一切時任運而起。常在前故。(d) 四者名爲智識。謂分別染淨法故。(e) 五者名爲相續識。以念相應不斷故。住持過去無量世等善惡之業。令不失故。復能成熟現在未來苦樂等報。無差違故。能令現在已經之事。忽然而念。未來之事。不覺妄慮。是故三

界虛僞唯心所作。離心則無六塵境界。此義云何、以一切法皆從心起。妄念而生。一切分別、卽分別自心、心不見心。無相可得、當知世間一切境界。皆依衆生無明妄心而得住持、是故一切法、如鏡中像無體可得、唯心虛妄以心生則種種法生。心滅則種種法滅故。

復次言意識者。卽此相續識。依諸凡夫取著轉深、計我我所。種種妄執、隨事攀緣。分別六塵、名爲意識。亦名分離識。又復說名分別事識、此識依見愛煩惱增長義故。

依無明熏習所起識者、非凡夫能知。亦非二乘智慧所覺、謂依菩薩。從初正信發心觀察。若證法身得少分知。乃至菩薩究竟地、不能盡知。唯佛窮

了。何以故。是心從本已來自性清淨。而有無明。爲無明所染。有其染心。雖
有染心。而常恒不變。是故此義唯佛能知。所謂心性常無念。故名爲不變。
以不達一法界故。心不相應。忽然念起。名爲無明。染心者有六種。云何爲
(a)(b) 六。一者執相應染。依二乘解脫及信相應地遠離故。二者不斷相應染。依
(c) 信相應地。修學方便。漸漸能捨。得淨心地究竟離故。三者分別智相應染。
(d) 依具戒地漸離。乃至無相方便地究竟離故。四者現色不相應染。依色自
(e)(f) 在地能離故。五者能見心不相應染。依心自在地能離故。六者根本業不
相應染。依菩薩盡地。得入如來地能離故。不了一法界義者。從信相應地
觀察學斷。入淨心地隨分得離。乃至如來地能究竟離故。言相應義者。謂

心念法異依染淨差別。而知相緣相同故。不相應義者。謂卽心不覺常無別異。不同知相緣相故。又染心義者。名爲煩惱礙。能障眞如根本智故。無明義者。名爲智礙。能障世間自然業智故。此義云何。以依染心能見能現妄取境界違平等性故。以一切法常靜無有起相。無明不覺妄與法違故。不能得隨順世間一切境界種種知故。

復次分別生滅相者有二種。云何爲二。一者麤與心相應故。二者細與心不相應故。又麤中之麤凡夫境界。麤中之細及細中之麤菩薩境界。細中之細。是佛境界。此二種生滅依於無明熏習而有。所謂依因依緣。依因者。不覺義故。依緣者。妄作境界義故。若因滅則緣滅。因滅故不相應心滅。緣

滅故相應心滅。問曰。若心滅者。云何相續。若相續者。云何說究竟滅。答曰。
所言滅者。唯心相滅非心體滅。如風依水而有動相。若水滅者則風相斷
絕無所依止。以水不滅風相相續。唯風滅故動相隨滅非是水滅。無明亦
爾依心體而動。若心體滅者。則衆生斷絕無所依止。以體不滅。心得相續。
唯癡滅故心相隨滅。非心智滅。

復次有四種法熏習義故染法淨法起不斷絕。云何爲四。一者淨法。名爲
眞如。二者一切染因名爲無明。三者妄心名爲業識。四者妄境界所謂六
塵。熏習義者。如世間衣服實無於香。若人以香而熏習故則有香氣。此
亦如是。眞如淨法。實無於染。但以無明而熏習故。則有染相。無明染法。實

aa

(a) bb cc (b)

無淨業。但以眞如而熏習故。則有淨用。云何熏習起染法不斷。所謂以依
眞如法故有於無明。以有無明染法因故即熏習眞如。以熏習故則有妄
心。以有妄心。即熏習無明不了眞如法故。不覺念起現妄境界以有妄境
界染法緣故。即熏習妄心。令其念著造種種業受於一切身心等苦。此妄
境界熏習義。則有二種。云何爲二。一者增長念熏習。二者增長取熏習。妄
心熏習義有二種。云何爲二。一者業識根本熏習。能受阿羅漢辟支佛一
切菩薩生滅苦故。二者增長分別事識熏習。能受凡夫業繫苦故。無明熏
習義有二種。云何爲二。一者根本熏習。以能成就業識義故。二者所起見
愛熏習。以能成就分別事識義故。云何熏習起淨法不斷。所謂以有眞如

(aa) bb aa

法故。能熏習無明。以熏習因緣力故。則令妄心厭生死苦樂求涅槃。以此妄心有厭求因緣故。卽熏習眞如、自信己性、知心妄動無前境界、修遠離法。以如實知無前境界故。種種方便起隨順行、不取不念。乃至久遠熏習力故。無明則滅。以無明滅故。心無有起。以無起故。境界隨滅。以因緣俱滅故。心相皆盡。名得涅槃成自然業。妄心熏習義有二種。云何爲二。一者分別事識熏習。依諸凡夫二乘人等厭生死苦、隨力所能。以漸趣向無上道故。二者意熏習。謂諸菩薩發心勇猛速趣涅槃故。眞如熏習義有二種。云何爲二。一者自體相熏習。二者用熏習。自體相熏習者。從無始世來具無漏法。備有不思議業。作境界之性。依此二義恒常熏習。以有熏習力故。能

令衆生、厭生死苦。樂求涅槃。自信己身有眞如法。發心修行。問曰。若如是義者、一切衆生、悉有眞如。等皆熏習。云何有信無信無量前後差別。皆應一時自知有眞如法、勤修方便等入涅槃。答曰。眞如本一。而有無量無邊無明。從本已來自性差別。厚薄不同故。過恒河沙等上煩惱依無明起差別。我見愛染煩惱。依無明起差別、如是一切煩惱依於無明所起。前後無量差別。唯如來能知故又諸佛法有因有緣。因緣具足。乃得成辨。如木中火性。是火正因。若無人知、不假方便能自燒木、無有是處。衆生亦爾。雖有正因熏習之力。若不遇諸佛菩薩善知識等以之爲緣。能自斷煩惱。入涅槃者。則無是處。若雖有外緣之力。而內淨法未有熏習力者。亦不能究竟

厭生死苦樂求涅槃。若因緣具足者。所謂自有熏習之力。又爲諸佛菩薩等慈悲願護故。能起厭苦之心。信有涅槃修習善根。以修善根成熟故。則値諸佛菩薩示敎利喜。乃能進趣向涅槃道。用熏習者。卽是衆生外緣之力。如是外緣有無量義。略說二種。云何爲二。一者差別緣。二者平等緣。差別緣者。此人依於諸佛菩薩等。從初發意始求道時。乃至得佛。於中若見若念。或爲眷屬父母諸親。或爲給使。或爲知友。或爲寃家。或起四攝。乃至一切所作無量行緣。以起大悲熏習之力。能令衆生增長善根。若見若聞。得利益故。此緣有二種。云何爲二。一者近緣。速得度故。二者遠緣。久遠得度故。是近遠二緣。分別復有二種。云何爲二。一者增長行緣。二者受道緣。

bbb 平等緣者。一切諸佛菩薩。皆願度脫一切衆生。自然熏習。恒常不捨。以同
體智力故。隨應見聞而現作業。所謂衆生依於三昧。乃得平等見諸佛故。
(cc) 此體用熏習。分別復有二種。云何爲二。一者未相應。謂凡夫二乘。初發意
菩薩等。以意意識熏習。依信力故。而能修行。未得無分別心與體相應故。
未得自在業修行與用相應故。二者已相應。謂法身菩薩。得無分別心。與
諸佛自體相應。得自在業。與諸佛智用相應。唯依法力。自然修行。熏習眞
(e) 如。滅無明故。復次染法。從無始已來。熏習不斷。乃至得佛。後則有斷。淨法
熏習。則無有斷。盡於未來。此義云何。以眞如法常熏習故。妄心則滅。法身
顯現。起用熏習。故無有斷。

復次。眞如自體相者。一切凡夫。聲聞。緣覺。菩薩。諸佛。無有增減。非前際生。非後際滅。畢竟常恒。從本已來。自性滿足一切功德。所謂自體有大智慧光明義故。徧照法界義故。眞實識知義故。自性淸淨心義故。常樂我淨義故。淸涼不變自在義故。具足如是過於恒沙不離不斷不異不思議佛法。乃至滿足無有所少義。故名爲如來藏。亦名如來法身。問曰。上說眞如其體平等離一切相。云何復說體有如是種種功德。答曰。雖實有此諸功德義。而無差別之相。等同一味。唯一眞如。此義云何。以無分別離分別相。是故無二。復以何義得說差別。以依業識生滅相示。此云何示。以一切法本來唯心實無於念。而有妄心不覺起念見諸境界故說無明。心性不起。即

是大智慧光明義故。若心起見。則有不見之相。心性離見。卽是徧照法界義故、若心有動。非眞識知。無有自性。非常非樂非我非淨。熱惱衰變則不自在。乃至具有過恒沙等妄染之義。對此義故。心性無動。則有過恒沙等諸淨功德相義示現、若心有起。更見前法可念者。則有所少。如是淨法無量功德。卽是一心。更無所念。是故滿足。名爲法身如來之藏。

復次。眞如用者。所謂諸佛如來。本在因地。發大慈悲、修諸波羅密。攝化衆生。立大誓願。盡欲度脫等衆生界。亦不限劫數。盡於未來、以取一切衆生如己身故。而亦不取衆生相。此以何義。謂如實知一切衆生及與己身。眞如平等無別異故。以有如是大方便智。除滅無明。見本法身。自然而有不

思議業種種之用。卽與眞如等徧一切處。又亦無有用相可得。何以故。謂
諸佛如來唯是法身智相之身。第一義諦無有世諦境界。離於施作。但隨
(a) 衆生見聞得益故說爲用。此用有二種。云何爲二。一者依分別事識。凡夫
二乘心所見者。名爲應身。以不知轉識現故。見從外來。取色分齊。不能盡
(b) 知故。二者依於業識。謂諸菩薩從初發意乃至菩薩究竟地心所見者名
爲報身。身有無量色。色有無量相。相有無量好。所住依果亦有無量種種
莊嚴。隨所示現。卽無有邊。不可窮盡。離分齊相。隨其所應。常能住持不毀
不失。如是功德。皆因諸波羅密等無漏行熏及不思議熏之所成就。具足
(c) 無量樂相故。說爲報身。又爲凡夫所見者。是其麤色。隨於六道各見不同。

(d) 種種異類非受樂相故說爲應身。復次。初發意菩薩所見者。以深信眞如
法故。少分而見。知彼色相莊嚴等事無來無去離於分齊唯依心現不離
眞如。然此菩薩猶自分別。以未入法身位故若得淨心。所見微妙其用轉
勝。乃至菩薩地盡。見之究竟。若離業識。則無見相以諸佛法身。無有彼此
(e) 色相迭相見故。問曰。若諸佛法身離於色相者。云何能現色相。答曰。即此
法身是色體故。能現於色。所謂從本已來色心不二。以色性卽智故。色體
無形說名智身。以智性卽色故。說名法身徧一切處。所現之色。無有分齊。
隨心能示。十方世界。無量菩薩。無量報身。無量莊嚴各各差別。皆無分齊。
而不相妨。此非心識分別能知。以眞如自在用義故。

復次顯示從生滅門卽入眞如門所謂推求五陰色之與心六塵境界畢竟無念以心無形相十方求之終不可得如人迷故謂東爲西方實不轉衆生亦爾無明迷故謂心爲念心實不動若能觀察知心無起卽得隨順入眞如門故

對治邪執者一切邪執皆依我見若離於我則無邪執是我見有二種云何爲二一者人我見二者法我見人我見者依諸凡夫說有五種云何爲五一者聞修多羅說如來法身畢竟寂寞猶如虛空以不知爲破著故卽謂虛空是如來性云何對治明虛空相是其妄法體無不實以對色故有是可見相令心生滅以一切色法本來是心實無外色若無色者則無虛

空之相、所謂一切境界唯心妄起故有。若心離於妄動。則一切境界滅。唯

b 一眞心無不徧。此謂如來廣大性智究竟之義。非如虛空相故。二者聞修

多羅說世間諸法畢竟體空。乃至涅槃眞如之法。亦畢竟空。從本已來自

空離一切相。以不知爲破著故、卽謂眞如涅槃之性唯是其空。云何對治。

c 明眞如法身自體不空。具足無量性功德故。三者聞修多羅說如來之藏

無有增減。體備一切功德之法、以不解故。卽謂如來之藏有色心法自相

差別。云何對治。以唯依眞如義說故。因生滅染如示現說差別故、四者聞

d 修多羅說一切世間生死染法皆依如來藏而有。一切諸法不離眞如。以

不解故、謂如來藏自體具有一切世間生死等法、云何對治。以如來藏從

本已來唯有過恒沙等諸淨功德不離不斷不異眞如義故。以過恒沙等煩惱染法唯是妄有性自本無。從無始世來未曾與如來藏相應故。若如來藏體有妄法而使證會永息妄者。則無有是處。五者。聞修多羅說依如來藏故有生死。依如來藏故得涅槃。以不解故。謂衆生有始。以見始故。復謂如來所得涅槃有其終盡還作衆生。云何對治。以如來藏無前際故。無明之相亦無有始。若說三界外更有衆生始起者。即是外道經說。又如來藏無有後際。諸佛所得涅槃。與之相應則無後際故。法我見者。依二乘鈍根故。如來但爲說人無我。以說不究竟。見有五陰生滅之法。怖畏生死妄取涅槃。云何對治。以五陰法自性不生。則無有滅。本來涅槃故。

復次。究竟離妄執者。當知染法淨法皆悉相待無有自相可說。是故一切法。從本已來。非色非心。非智非識。非有非無。畢竟不可說相。而有言說者。

G 當知如來善巧方便。假以言說引導衆生。其旨趣者。皆爲離念歸於眞如。以念一切法令心生滅不入實智故。

B 分別發趣道相者。謂一切諸佛所證之道。一切菩薩發心修行趣向義故。略說發心有三種。云何爲三、一者信成就發心。二者解行發心。三者證發心。

1 信成就發心者。依何等人。修何等行。得信成就。堪能發心。所謂依不定聚衆生有熏習善根力故。信業果報能起十善。厭生死苦。欲求無上菩提。得値諸佛。親承供養修行信心。經一萬劫。信心成就故。諸佛菩薩敎令發

心。或以大悲故能自發心。或因正法欲滅。以護法因緣。能自發心。如是信
a 心成就得發心者。入正定聚。畢竟不退。名住如來種中正因相應。若有衆
生。善根微少。久遠已來煩惱深厚。雖値於佛。亦得供養。然起人天種子。或
起二乘種子。設有求大乘者。根則不定。若進若退。或有供養諸佛。未經一
萬劫。於中遇緣。亦有發心。所謂見佛色相而發其心。或因供養衆僧而發
其心。或因二乘之人教令發心。或學他發心。如是等發心。悉皆不定。遇惡
b 因緣。或便退失。墮二乘地。復次信成就發心者。發何等心。略說有三種。云
何爲三。一者直心。正念眞如法故。二者深心。樂集一切善諸行故。三者大
悲心。欲拔一切衆生苦故。問曰。上說法界一相。佛體無二。何故不唯念眞

如。復假求學諸善之行。答曰。譬如大摩尼寶體性明淨而有鑛穢之垢若人雖念寶性不以方便種種磨治終無得淨。如是衆生眞如之法。體性空淨。而有無量煩惱垢染。若人雖念眞如。不以方便種種熏修亦無得淨。以垢無量無邊徧一切法故修一切善行以爲對治。若人修行一切善法。自然歸順眞如法故。略說方便有四種。云何爲四。(1)一者行根本方便。謂觀一切法自性無生。離於妄見。不住生死。觀一切法因緣和合業果不失。起於大悲。修諸福德。攝化衆生。不住涅槃。以隨順法性無住故。(2)二者能止方便。(3)謂慚愧悔過。能止一切惡法。不令增長。以隨順法性離諸過故。三者發起善根增長方便。謂勤供養禮拜三寶。讚歎隨喜勸請諸佛。以愛敬三寶淳

厚心故。信得增長。乃能志求無上之道。又因佛法僧力所護故。能消業障
(4) 善根不退。以隨順法性離癡障故。四者大願平等方便。所謂發願盡於未
來。化度一切衆生。使無有餘。皆令究竟無餘涅槃。以隨順法性無斷絕故。
d 法性廣大。徧一切衆生。平等無二。不念彼此。究竟寂滅故。菩薩發是心故。
則得少分見法身。以見法身故。隨其願力。能現八種利益衆生。所謂從兜
率天退。入胎。住胎。出胎。出家。成道。轉法輪。入於涅槃。然是菩薩未名法身。
以其過去無量世來有漏之業。未能決斷。隨其所生。與微苦相應。亦非業
e 繫。以有大願自在力故。如修多羅中。或說有退墮惡趣者。非其實退。但爲
f 初學菩薩未入正位而懈怠者。恐怖令彼勇猛故。又是菩薩一發心後。遠

2 離怯弱。畢竟不畏墮二乘地。若聞無量無邊阿僧祇劫勤苦難行。乃得湼
槃。亦不怯弱。以信知一切法從本已來自湼槃故。解行發心者。當知轉勝。
以是菩薩從初正信已來。於第一阿僧祇劫將欲滿故。於眞如法中。深解
a b 現前。所修離相。以知法性體無慳貪故。隨順修行檀波羅蜜。以知法性無
c 染離五欲過故。隨順修行尸波羅蜜。以知法性無苦離瞋惱故。隨順修行
d 羼提波羅蜜。以知法性無身心相離懈怠故。隨順修行毗梨耶波羅蜜。以
e f 知法性常定體無亂故。隨順修行禪波羅蜜。以知法性體明離無明故。隨
3 順修行般若波羅蜜。證發心者。從淨心地。乃至菩薩究竟地。證何境界。所
謂眞如。以依轉識說爲境界。而此證者。無有境界。唯眞如智名爲法身。是

a 菩薩於一念頃。能至十方無餘世界。供養諸佛。請轉法輪。唯爲開導利益衆生。不依文字。或示超地速成正覺。以爲怯弱衆生故。或說我於無量阿僧祇劫當成佛道。以爲懈慢衆生故。能示如是無數方便。不可思議。而實菩薩種種根等。發心則等。所證亦等。無有超過之法。以一切菩薩皆經三阿僧祇劫故。b 但隨衆生世界不同。所見所聞根欲性異。故示所行亦有差別、又是菩薩發心相者。有三種心微細之相。云何爲三。一者眞心無分別故。c 二者方便心自然徧行利益衆生故。三者業識心微細起滅故。又是菩薩功德成滿。於色究竟處。示一切世間最高大身。謂以一念相應慧。無明頓盡。名一切種智、自然而有不思議業。能現十方利益衆生。問曰。虛空無

9.Q 邊故。世界無邊。世界無邊故。衆生無邊。衆生無邊故。心行差別亦復無邊。
如是境界不可分齊。難知難解。若無明斷。無有心想。云何能了。名一切種
智。答曰。一切境界本來一心。離於想念。以衆生妄見境界故。心有分齊。以
妄起想念不稱法性故。不能決了。諸佛如來離於見想無所不徧。心眞實
故。卽是諸法之性。自體顯照一切妄法。有大智用無量方便。隨諸衆生所
10Q 應得解。皆能開示種種法義。是故得名一切種智。又問曰。若諸佛有自然
業。能現一切處利益衆生者。一切衆生若見其身。若覩神變。若聞其說。無
不得利。云何世間多不能見。答曰。諸佛如來法身平等徧一切處。無有作
意故。說自然。但依衆生心現。衆生心者。猶如於鏡。鏡若有垢。色像不現。如

是衆生心若有垢法身不現故。

已說解釋分。次說修行信心分。

是中依未入正定聚衆生故說修行信心。何等信心。云何修行。略說信心有四種。云何爲四。一者信根本。所謂樂念眞如法故。二者信佛有無量功德。常念親近供養恭敬發起善根。願求一切智故。三者信法有大利益。常念修行諸波羅蜜故。四者信僧能正修行自利利他。常樂親近諸菩薩衆。求學如實行故。修行有五門。能成此信。云何爲五。一者施門。二者戒門。三者忍門。四者進門。五者止觀門。云何修行施門。若見一切來求索者。所有財物隨力施與。以自捨慳貪。令彼歡喜。若見厄難恐怖危逼。隨己堪任。施

與無畏。若有衆生來求法者。隨己能解。方便爲說。不應貪求名利恭敬。唯
B 念自利利他迴向菩提故。云何修行戒門。所謂不殺不盜不婬不兩舌不
惡口不妄言不綺語。遠離貪嫉欺詐諂曲瞋恚邪見。若出家者。爲折伏煩
惱故。亦應遠離憒鬧。常處寂靜。修習少欲知足頭陀等行。乃至小罪心生
怖畏。慚愧改悔。不得輕於如來所制禁戒。當護譏嫌不令衆生妄起過罪
C 故。云何修行忍門。所謂應忍他人之惱心不懷報。亦當忍於利衰毀譽稱
D 譏苦樂等法故。云何修行進門。所謂於諸善事心不懈退。立志堅強遠離
怯弱。當念過去久遠已來虛受一切身心大苦無有利益。是故應勤修諸
功德自利利他速離衆苦。復次若人雖修行信心以從先世來多有重罪

惡業障故。爲邪魔諸鬼之所惱亂。或爲世間事務種種牽纏。或爲病苦所惱。有如是等衆多障礙。是故應當勇猛精勤晝夜六時禮拜諸佛誠心懺悔勸請隨喜迴向菩提。常不休廢。得免諸障。善根增長故。云何修行止觀門。所言止者。謂止一切境界相隨順奢摩他觀義故。所言觀者。謂分別因緣生滅相隨順毘鉢舍那觀義故。云何隨順以此二義。漸漸修習不相捨離。雙現前故。若修止者。住於靜處端坐正意。不依氣息。不依形色。不依於空。不依地水火風。乃至不依見聞覺知。一切諸想隨念皆除。亦遣除想。以一切法本來無想。念念不生。念念不滅。亦常不得隨心外念境界後以心除心。心若馳散。即當攝來住於正念。是正念者。當知唯心無外境界。即復

[a] 此心亦無自相。念念不可得。若從坐起。去來進止有所施作。於一切時。常念方便。隨順觀察。久習淳熟其心得住。以心住故。漸漸猛利。隨順得入眞如三昧。深伏煩惱。信心增長。速成不退。唯除疑惑。不信誹謗。重罪業障。我[b] 慢懈怠。如是等人。所不能入。復次。依是三昧故。則知法界一相。謂一切諸佛法身與衆生身平等無二。卽名一行三昧。當知眞如是三昧根本。若人[e] 修行漸漸能生無量三昧。或有衆生無善根力。則爲諸魔外道鬼神之所惑亂。若於坐中現形恐怖。或現端正男女等相。當念唯心。境界則滅。終不爲惱。或現天像菩薩像。亦作如來像。相好具足。若說陀羅尼。若說布施持戒忍辱精進禪定智慧。或說平等空無相無願無怨無親無因無果畢竟

空寂是眞涅槃。或令人知宿命過去之事。亦知未來之事得他心智辯才無礙。能令衆生貪著世間名利之事又令使人數瞋數喜性無常準。或多慈愛多睡多病。其心懈怠或卒起精進、後便休廢生於不信。多疑多慮。或捨本勝行。更修雜行、若著世事。種種牽纏。亦能使人得諸三昧少分相似皆是外道所得非眞三昧。或復令人若一日若二日若三日乃至七日。住於定中。得自然香美飲食身心適悅。不飢不渴、使人愛著、或亦令人食無分齊、乍多乍少。顏色變異。以是義故。行者常應智慧觀察勿令此心墮邪網。當勤正念不取不著則能遠離是諸業障、應知外道所有三昧皆不離見愛我慢之心貪著世間名利恭敬故。眞如三昧者。不住見相。不住得相。

乃至出定亦無懈慢。所有煩惱漸漸微薄。若諸凡夫不習此三昧法。得入如來種性。無有此處。以修世間諸禪三昧。多起味著。依於我見。繫屬三界。與外道共。若離善知識所護。則起外道見。故復次精勤專心修學此三昧者。現世當得十種利益。云何爲十。一者常爲十方諸佛菩薩之所護念。二者不爲諸魔惡鬼所能恐怖。三者不爲九十五種外道鬼神之所惑亂。四者遠離誹謗甚深之法。重罪業障漸漸微薄。五者滅一切疑諸惡覺觀。六者於如來境界信得增長。七者遠離憂悔。於生死中勇猛不怯。八者其心柔和捨於憍慢。不爲他人所惱。九者雖未得定。於一切時一切境界處。則能減損煩惱。不樂世間。十者若得三昧。不爲外緣一切音聲之所驚動。

2 ab c d e f g

復次。若人唯修於止。則心沈沒。或起懈怠。不樂衆善。遠離大悲。是故修觀。修習觀者。當觀一切世間有爲之法。無得久停。須臾變壞。一切心行。念念生滅。以是故苦。應觀過去所念諸法。恍惚如夢。應觀現在所念諸法。猶如電光。應觀未來所念諸法。猶如於雲。欻爾而起。應觀世間一切有身。悉皆不淨。種種穢汙。無一可樂。如是當念。一切衆生。從無始世來。皆因無明所熏習故。令心生滅。已受一切身心大苦。現在卽有無量逼迫。未來所苦。亦無分齊。難捨難離。而不覺知。衆生如是。甚爲可愍。作是思惟。卽應勇猛立大誓願。願令我心離分別故。徧於十方。修行一切諸善功德。盡其未來。以無量方便。救拔一切苦惱衆生。令得涅槃第一義樂。以起如是願故。於一

3 切時一切處。所有衆善。隨己堪能。不捨修學。心無懈怠。唯除坐時專念於止。若餘一切。悉當觀察應作不應作。

若行若住若坐若臥若起。皆應止觀俱行。所謂雖念諸法自性不生。而復卽念因緣和合善惡之業。苦樂等報。不失不壞。雖念因緣善惡業報。而亦卽念性不可得。若修止者。對治凡夫住著世間。能捨二乘怯弱之見。若修觀者。對治二乘不起大悲狹劣心過。遠離凡夫不修善根。以此義故。是止觀門。共相助成。不相捨離。若止觀不具。則無能入菩提之道。

4 復次。衆生初學是法。欲求正信。其心怯弱。以住於此娑婆世界。自畏不能常直諸佛親承供養。懼謂信心難可成就。意欲退者。當知如來有勝方便。

攝護信心。謂以專意念佛因緣。隨願得生他方佛土。常見於佛。永離惡道、如修多羅說、若人專念西方極樂世界阿彌陀佛。所修善根迴向。願求生彼世界。卽得往生。常見佛故。終無有退、若觀彼佛眞如法身常勤修習。畢竟得生住正定故。

已說修行信心分。次說勸修利益分、

如是摩訶衍。諸佛秘藏。我已總說。若有衆生。欲於如來甚深境界得生正信遠離誹謗入大乘道。當持此論思量修習究竟能至無上之道。若人聞是法已不生怯弱。當知此人定紹佛種。必爲諸佛之所授記。假使有人能化三千大千世界滿中衆生。令行十善。不如有人於一食頃正思此法。過

D 前功德。不可爲喻。復次若人受持此論。觀察修。行若一日一夜所有功德。
無量無邊不可得說。假令十方一切諸佛。各於無量無邊阿僧祇劫、歎其
功德。亦不能盡。何以故。謂法性功德無有盡故。此人功德。亦復如是。無有
E 邊際。其有衆生。於此論中毀謗不信。所獲罪報。經無量劫。受大苦惱、是故
衆生。但應仰信。不應誹謗。以深自害。亦害他人。斷絕一切三寶之種、以一
F 切如來皆依此法得涅槃故。一切菩薩因之修行入佛智故、當知過去菩
薩。已依此法。得成淨信。現在菩薩。今依此法、得成淨信。未來菩薩。當依此
法。得成淨信。是故衆生。應勤修學。

諸佛甚深廣大義　我今隨分總持說